Beverly Pagram was educated at Greycoats, Westminster, and the University of Western Australia. After a five-year stint as Women's Editor of Australia's largest Sunday paper she returned to England, where her journalistic career has included writing for many national newspapers and magazines. Her interests include organic gardening, exotic cooking and writing short stories. In addition to *Heaven and Hearth*, Beverly has written a book on folkloric and herbal household hints entitled *Natural Housekeeping – Rediscovered Recipes for Home and Care* (Gaia Books). She lives in a decayed eighteenth-century house in Oxfordshire with her scriptwriter husband, two daughters and five ravenous cats.

heaven & hearth

A Seasonal Compendium of Women's
Spiritual & Domestic Lore

BEVERLY PAGRAM

First published by The Women's Press Ltd, 1997
A member of the Namara Group
34 Great Sutton Street, London EC1V 0DX

British Library Cataloguing-in-Data
A catalogue record for this book is available from the British Library

ISBN 0 7043 4540 4

Typeset in Goudy Old Style by Intype
Printed and bound in Great Britain by CPD (Wales) Ltd

Acknowledgements

The author would like to thank Martin Orskey sincerely for allowing her access to his collection of rare antiquarian domestic and gardening books; and Christine Green for lending her *The Housekeeping Book of the Saunders Family Women*.

To my mother

Contents

Introduction

I read it [history] a little as a duty; but it tells me nothing that does not either vex or weary me. The quarrels of popes and kings, with wars and pestilences on every page; the men all so good for nothing, and hardly any women at all, it is very tiresome...

Catherine Morland in *Northanger Abbey*,
Jane Austen, 1818

Our English housewife must be of chaste thought, stout courage, patient, untired, watchful, diligent, witty, pleasant, constant in friendship, full of good neighbourhood, wise in discourse, but not frequent therein ... comfortable in her counsels, and generally skilful in all the worthy knowledge which do belong to her vocation.

The English Hus-wife, Gervase Markham, 1615

For everything there is a season, and a time to every
   purpose under heaven:
a time to be born, and a time to die;
a time to plant and a time to pluck up
   that which is planted.

Ecclesiastes

O, who can tell the hidden power of herbs, and might of
magic spell?

Edmund Spenser

And what is bettre than wisedoom? Womman.
And what is bettre than a good womman?
Nothyng.

The Canterbury Tales, Geoffrey Chaucer

his book aims to restore a 'lost' portion of women's history: to open a dusty cupboard in our collective psyche and let loose a cavalcade of ignored ghosts, female shamans and shadowy goddesses. Once upon a time girls were initiated at their mothers' and grandmothers' knees into the archaic traditions and aesthetics of household management. The geography of scattered families and the politics of emancipation have put paid to that. However, even in the most liberated Western domestic sphere the 'mistress of the house' inherits, unwitting or not, an arcane feminine culture drawing on occultism, alchemy, astrology, herbalism, and pagan worship of The Great Mother/Madonna and her symbolic representative, the moon. In undervaluing this housewifely omniscience of yesteryear, it seems to me we are blocking an important backlog of women's folk memory.

Since antiquity women have measured their existences with a complex network of gender-specific behaviour patterns and beliefs. Day-to-day 'housework' has been punctuated by a rich mystical interior life. This usually took the form of the 'intuitive' wisdom of the unconscious mind and an array of rituals enmeshed in an intricate web of folklore, religion and superstition. In the days of ancient Rome, for example, no woman of any class would dream of starting her daily tasks without offerings to Vesta, deity of the hearth, and her other lesser *lares et penates* – household gods.

Female work in the home has been consistently undervalued by scholarship and society alike. Yet in European pre-industrial rural areas the daily tasks which faced individual women embraced a bewildering variety of specialist crafts and skills, among them spinning, preserving, brewing, gardening, dyeing, apiary, animal husbandry, sewing, plus working in the stillroom on lotions, potions and distillations used for family physic and a myriad other purposes. All this in between cooking, childcare and any outside employment! The only way such a workload could be borne in a paternalistic society was through a strong co-operative support network of friends, relatives and neighbours in a self-reliant community of women.

> First in the morning when thou art waked and purporest to ryse, lyft up thy hands and bless thee and make a sign of holy cross, and if thou says a Paternoster and Ave and a Crede and remember thy maker, thou shall speed moche the better. And when thou arte up and redy, then first swepe thy house, dress up thy dysshe borde, and set all thynge in good order within thy house, milk thy kyne, sockle thy calves, sye up thy mylke, take up thy chyldre, and arraye them, and proudye for thy husbandes brekefaste, dyher, souper and for thy chyldren, and servantes.
>
> Beginning of 'A Womman's Day', from the
> *Boke of Husbandry*, Sir Anthony Fitzherbert, 1525

The myriad responsibilities of economic and social administration also fell frequently to the housewife in larger wealthier households (castles, mansions, large townhouses and farms) in England during the medieval, Tudor and Elizabethan periods. It was common for these women, when they could read and write, to keep massive 'household books' in which they wrote everything from the cost of salt that season to new recipes and a cure for earache they had heard from a friend. It was these painstaking handwritten compendiums and their wide-ranging observations which were often 'borrowed' wholesale or used as source material by the burgeoning male-dominated new publishing industry of the late sixteenth and seventeenth centuries. Thus the inclusion in this book of quotes from male authors of the day on a variety of domestic subjects – they reflect the archive of women's household jottings, intuition and advice which inspired them. I've also included a small scattering of daft sexist quotes – from *The Old Bridal Calendar*, both for entertainment and to remind us how crude female stereotyping could (and can!) be.

The title *Heaven and Hearth* was inspired by the fact that

along with the practical observations and recipes passed down from generation to generation, orally in the case of poorer women, came an avalanche of what are often dismissed as 'old wives' tales'. Some were granny-cosy; some were downright witchy, emanating from the eerie psychic borderlands of folklore and superstition.

There were strange cakes for even stranger saints' festivals, quaint nostrums, magic formulations, wisewoman healing rhymes, and intricate rules regarding plants and celestial influences direct from Hecate in her magic garden at Colchis. Our housewifely ancestors, far from being mundane, were independently spiritual, 'domystic' even, in the domestic sphere. I wanted this book to be a flavoursome 'taster', a gallimaufry of that richly fascinating hidden past that is northern European women's heritage.

With the focus mainly on northern Europe, the backdrop is necessarily that of the Roman and Celtic pagan and Christian-based cultures which have interwoven over the centuries to form an intricate pattern of beliefs and behaviours. In restoring the potent, spirit-filled subculture of country women's lore, daily devotions, divinations, purification rites and talismans, I have set out the material in a monthly format travelling through the seasons of the year – showing how important changes in the weather and nature were to the daily lives of women in the past.

Their cyclical biology has always given women a special link with the natural world (a biological bond which also constantly threatened their lives through the dangers of the birth process), and in early cultures caused them to be venerated because of their mysterious body magic. The visionary medieval German nun and herbalist Hildegarde of Bingen wrote reverently from her '*hortus conclusus*' (an enclosed garden, a metaphor for the soul), of a power she felt empathy with – something she called '*viriditas*': the 'greening power', in essence the mystic force of nature's regeneration.

In *The Golden Bough* anthropologist Sir James Frazer noted: 'The ancient Germans believed there was something holy in women, and accordingly consulted them as oracles.' It was their direct link with divinity/regeneration through the life cycle which in the past gave women complete autonomy in the home where the practicalities and cult rituals to do with birth and death were concerned. This natural association also promoted in women forms of ancestor-worship and a whole canon of belief in a wide range of supernatural beings and psychic fauna. Many women – not only clairvoyants – regularly told fortunes by their firesides using tea-leaves, cards or scrying balls. The areas of love and sex were particularly rich in auguries and luck-bringing votive amulets, some of which are still extant in Europe.

Inexplicable household mysteries such as the 'sacred' placement of objects, one's natural veneration of the hearth, the almost animistic authority of a much-used old kitchen implement, the overwhelming sense of *genius locii* – 'spirit of place' – all of these survive to some extent for many women today.

Domestic rites and beliefs mentioned in this book are therefore, where possible, put into historical or mythological context. A surprising amount of modern northern European popular culture is descended from pre-Christian (usually Celtic and/or Roman/Greek/Egyptian) ceremonies and customs. This 'telescoped' historical compendium necessarily has to generalise across the eras, but I hope it vividly brings to life the everyday enigmas of scores of forgotten women.

> Let me tell you this:
> Someone in some future
> Time will think of us.
>
> Sappho

NB: When some of the sources in this book were written, the Julian calendar was in use. When in 1752 the Gregorian calendar was introduced in Britain (it had been used in Catholic Europe for 170 years by then), there was a discrepancy of eleven days between the old and the 'new' style calendar. Readers should bear this almost fortnight's leap ahead in mind when reading the festival dates in this book.

The Months

January cold desolate;
February all dripping wet;
March wind ranges
April changes;
Birds sing in tune
To flowers of May,
And sunny June
Brings longest day;
In scorched July
The storm-clouds fly;
Lightning-torn August bears corn;
September fruit;
In rough October
Earth must disrobe her;
Stars fall and shoot
In keen November;
And night is long
And cold is strong
In bleak December.

Christina Rossetti

January

On the twelfth day of Christmas my true love
sent to me:
12 lords a-leaping, 11 ladies dancing,
10 pipers piping, 9 drummers drumming,
8 maids a-milking, 7 swans a-swimming,
6 geese a-laying, 5 gold rings,
4 calling birds, 3 French hens,
2 turtle doves, and a partridge in a pear tree.

Anon

Hail to the old apple-tree!
From every bough
Give us apples enow;
Hatsful, capsful,
Bushels and sacksful.
Even a little heap under the stairs!
Traditional West Country apple-tree wassail

What is love? 'tis not hereafter;
Present mirth hath present laughter;
What's to come is still unsure:
In delay there lies no plenty;

11

Then come and kiss me, sweet and twenty,
Youth's a stuff will not endure.

Clown song, *Twelfth Night*, William Shakespeare

To make a Twelfth Cake. Put two pounds of butter in a warm
pan and work it to a cream with your hand; then put in two
pounds of loaf sugar sifted; a large nutmeg grated; and of cinnamon ground, allspice ground, ginger, mace and coriander each a
quarter ounce. Now break in eighteen eggs by one and one,
meantime beating it for twenty minutes or above; stir in a gill of
brandy: then add two pounds of sifted flour, and work it a little.
Next put in currants four pounds, chopped almonds half a
pound; citron the like; and orange and lemon peel cut small half
a pound. Put in one bean and one pea in separate places, bake it
in a slow oven for four hours, and ice it and decorate it as you
will.

The Experienced English Housekeeper, Elizabeth Raffald, 1769

The first change of the new moon in the new year; the first
time you see, hold your hands across, saying this three times:
New Moon, new moon, prithee tell me this night who my
true love will be.

Mother Bunch's Closet, 1685

And turn, sole-thoughted, to one Lady there,
Whose heart had brooded, all that wintry day,
On love, and wing'd St Agnes' saintly care,
As she had heard old dames full many times declare.
They told her how, upon St Agnes Eve
Young virgins might have visions of delight
And soft adorings from their loves receive
Upon the honey'd middle of the night,
If ceremonies due they did aright...

The Eve of St Agnes, John Keats

Good Dame, here at your door
Our wassel we begin,
We are all maidens poor
We pray now let us in.

Women's Wassail, Anon

Women should restrain themselves with seemly conduct among knights and squires ... and, whether in dances or amusements, divert and amuse themselves decorously ... they must not go about with their heads raised like wild deer.

The Treasure of the City of Ladies, Christine de Pisan, 1405

Seed Water

Take a spoonful of Coriander Seed, half a spoonful of Caraway-Seed bruised, and boild in a Pint of Water, then Strain it, and bruise it up with the Yolk of an Egg, and so mix it with Sack and double-refined Sugar, according to your Palate.

Surfeit Mixture from *The Art of Cookery Made Plain and Easy*, Hannah Glasse, 1747

anuary is so named after the Roman god of doorways, Janus, who looks both back to the Old Year and forwards to the New. At the festival of Kalends, a jovial Roman mid-winter festival, which honoured Hera/Juno, worshippers offered vows to the goddess and gave each other presents of bay garlands and figs, honey, pastry and coins. Tudor, Elizabethan and Jacobean women fashioned gifts of embroidered gloves, pincushions, rowan-berry necklaces, and apples speared with rosemary and cloves. At Hogmanay in Scotland, triangular 'Trinity-shaped' shortbread oatcakes known as 'petticoat tails' (after Elizabethan gored skirt segments) were made and exchanged, along with homemade *uisquebaugh* (whisky). It was auspicious to leave a sample of both outside the house to appease the Banshee fairy-women, whose appetites were legendary.

Say no ill of the year, till it be past.

Proverb

On New Year's morning in medieval England, luck-seekers rose early to put up the pristine new calendar/almanac, which should under no account have been looked at before the First of January. Nothing was meant to be taken out of the house on New Year's Day until the (male) New Year luck-bringer had knocked on the door with coal, bread and a coin, even if he came very late! There are, however, tales of some daringly enterprising women overcoming this problem by putting their own lump of coal, crust and coin outside in the porch late on New Year's Eve, and just reaching out and bringing it back in on the stroke of midnight. Earlybird cleaners had to be careful – dust had to be swept towards the hearth for safety, in case any of the family's existing good fortune blew out of the door before the new had been officially ushered in.

15

The house had usually been made spick and span all the preceding week to welcome the year – the ashes raked out, floor-rushes changed, the hearth swept, and damp cellars dried by standing jars of salt in them. Feather mattresses were vigorously shaken, and a new-plucked white feather – 'the feather luck' – put inside the mattress case, as a symbol of reborn opportunity.

In parts of rural Scotland it was traditional to 'fumigate' the house with an incense of burning juniper to drive away the old year; a custom adopted by Elizabeth I, who insisted on this purification ritual in her bedchamber. Elsewhere, thick clean white curtains were hung at the windows if possible as a barrier to any lingering malign spirits, and the doorstep either freshly whitened or painted with new protective patterns. An ivy leaf was put in a saucer of water at the beginning of New Year's Day – if it was still fresh and uncurled by midnight this was a most auspicious sign. All visitors on the first day of the year had to leave by a different door to the one they came in, and it was deemed bad luck indeed for them to ask to borrow anything!

Lucky indeed was she who got to the local well first on New Year's morning – for the water she drew was known as 'Cream of the Well', which was thought to have amazing curative and cosmetic qualities. Later arrivals dropped silvery pins or small silver coins in the well to 'buy' some residual good luck and magical beautification for themselves.

During the Roman renewal feast of the epiphany of the mother goddess Demeter/Persephone, a divinatory bean was used to draw lots for who should be the leader of the proceedings. This ritual was the forerunner of the practice of choosing a 'King of the Bean and Queen of the Pea' for Twelfth Night and similar revels, common in parts of Europe until the late eighteenth century. The custom of putting 'lucky' charms into food during the Christmas season has been 'stolen' by the Christmas Day pudding in modern times. However, it was originally a Twelfth Night/Epiphany caper – in France the charms are in a *galette des rois* for the three Magi; in Italy they're sometimes found in January's *Befana* or 'witch' cake.

The Twelfth Night gambols started on the twelfth day after the celebration of the Nativity, and was the last feast at which the Christmas greenery decorations were still allowed. Disposal of them was, like everything else, governed by fortune-appeasement. For most housewives it was taboo to burn them; they went into the compost heap to fertilise the garden.

Disguise was the theme of the Twelfth – nothing was as it seemed. The medieval Queen of the Pea wore a green gown, a paper crown, and was masked like the rest of the assembly. She and the Bean King presided over a cavalcade of mumming, dancing and games directly descended from the forfeits and stylised merriment of Kalends. More recently this festival has taken a back seat to Christian Epiphany, which celebrates the manifestation of the Wise Men. On 6 January Victorian women vied with each other to make the most magnificent Epiphany Tarts, with complicated latticework and lozenge patterns and three different hued jams or preserves representing the Magi's gifts of gold, frankincense and myrrh.

A ceremony which lasted into this century, and has recently been revived in Somerset and Hereford, is the Twelfth Night Wassailing of Apple Trees. The ubiquitous Wassail Bowl of 'Lambswool', hot spiced cider with toast and crab-apples bobbing in it, was taken out into the apple-orchards, where a favourite old tree was sung to and a libation of cider was offered. Sometimes a cider-soaked cake would be left in the fork of a tree as a fertility offering for the growing season to come.

St Distaff Day on 7 January was not in fact a saint's day at all, but a commemoration of the day on which, every year, women returned to their distaffs of unspun wool to begin spinning again. A few days later, on 'Plough Monday', while the men returned once more to the fields, women made globes of woven hawthorn to hang from the rafters of their houses. Once a symbol of the Roman cult of Flora, this sacred Celtic tree, whose flowering heralded the festival of Beltane, was a favoured country emblem of vegetative renewal.

While the women made new globes the men burned the old

ones in the newly ploughed fields and scattered the hawthorn ash in the furrows to 'fertilise' the newly sown wheat.

Viola to Olivia: Make me a willow cabin at your gate,
And call upon my soul within the house...
Twelfth Night, William Shakespeare

Weaving dried willow wands into baskets and other receptacles was another women's job for this time of year, along with the collecting of thorns for domestic use. Classical mythology dedicates the willow to the Underworld, Moon, Hera, Circe and Hecate, so it was the plant of choice for binding witches' brooms – thence the origin of the word 'wicker' (wicca) for woven willow artefacts. This was also the chosen time for witches to make themselves new wands from long sprigs of yew, and indeed yew was used by some women to dowse the house for lost articles.

* * *

St Agnes' Day, on 20 January, honours a 13-year-old saintly maiden. According to legend the spirited youngster was sent to a bordello by Emperor Diocletian for refusing to give up her faith, but her cropped hair miraculously grew down to her feet overnight to cover her nakedness.

Fair St Agnes, play thy part
And send to me my own sweetheart
Traditional

St Agnes' Eve was a night hotly favoured by young women for love divination rituals in parts of England until early this century, despite the saint being the patron of chastity! Some women primed themselves for vivid dreams by eating lots of salted herrings and eggshells, some rather dangerously stuck 'magical' pins in their nightshirt sleeves before they went to bed walking backwards. Others sat silently making a 'Dumb Cake'.

This edible augury had to be made by two girls together using eggshells as measuring spoons, but the spell would be broken if either of them said a word or laughed. They had to prick their initials on top of the cake with a bodkin or pin, put the cake by the fire, and then wait until midnight for the objects of their desires to materialise at the door.

Other culinary exploits for January included making buns called Pope Ladies (so called because of their pointed, mitre-like shape). Tangy early salads and pickles were made from hawthorn buds; then there was carrot soup (much favoured also by Frenchwomen to allay infant stomach ailments and to apply to sore nipples); 'chewing gum' from honeycomb; prune pie; lentil stew (a popular New Year 'fertility' dish in Italy); cabbage and marrow turnovers, and leeks, leeks galore, for:

> Now leeks are in season, for pottage full good,
> And spareth the milch cow, and purgeth the blood.
>
> Traditional

Gentlewomen in charge of great houses had the onerous task of organising enormous feasts until the very end of the festive season, with all the dishes laid out on the table in complicated, pre-ordained sequences:

> She must first marshall her sallets, delivering the grand sallet first ... Next unto sallets she shall deliver foorth all her fricases ... after them all her boyld meats ... next to them all sorts of rost meates ... then bak't meats ... then lastly Carbonados [grilled meats], simple and compound.
>
> *The English Hus-wife*, Gervase Markham, 1615

Sweets of all sorts were devoured by those rich enough to afford the huge cone-shaped sugar loaves – imported from North Africa and the West Indies – that began to usurp honey after the medieval period. Knowing how to make 'banquetting stuffe' of candied fruit and vegetables was an essential art for the lady of the house, who often decorated her creations with birds, animals and heavenly bodies made of marchpane (marzipan) or sugar candy.

> *To Make Rocks of Cyttron, and Orenge,*
> *and Lemmon, and Angelica*
>
> Take of the Greenest tender Cyttron, and of the Preserved Angelica, and Orenge, and Lemmon; peel an equal Quantity; and cut them in small long pieces, and boyl as much Sugar ... till it will Rope: Then put in the before-mentioned Particulars; and boyl all together, till it will Candy: Then lay it out in Rocks upon Writing Paper.
>
> *The True Way of Preserving and Candying and*
> *Making Several Sorts of Sweet-Meats,*
> *According to the Best and Truest Manner –*
> *Made Public for the Benefit of all English*
> *Ladies and Gentlewomen*, Anon, 1695

* * *

Avoiding toothache, or worse still, wooden dentures, during this season of prolonged hospitality must have been difficult. Cavities were treated with clove oil and stoppered with garlic cloves, and sore gums rubbed with a rose and lavender salve or a paste of rose-hips. Bad breath was countered by chewing cinnamon sticks and caraway seeds, which last ingredient was the basis of an aromatic, freshening cordial called 'Oil of Venus' by French housewives.

Hot caraway bread stuffed into the ear was thought a sovereign kitchen physic remedy for ear-ache, and salt and lemon juice was recommended by Sir Hugh Platt (1605) in *Delightes For Ladies* as just the thing for a pimpled face brought about by festive excess. For that bane of heavy drinkers, gout, Hildegard of Bingen in the twelfth century proposed a fairly culinary concoction of powdered saxifrage, rue, nutmeg, cloves and celery seed. Beans were brought into play for those individuals struck down by mid-winter melancholy:

To Defend Humours

Take beans, the rind of the upper skin being pulled off, and bruise them and mingle them with the white of an egg. Make it stick to the temples; it keepeth back humours flowing to the eyes.

The Good Housewife's Jewell, Thomas Dawson, 1596

Winter backaches were warded off by the wearing of a pink tourmaline gem, a favourite of alchemists of old, somewhere on the upper torso. Many other January remedies came from the garden, where there were already encouraging signs of life amongst the silvered tracery of frosty stems and branches. Early hazel catkins and woodbine leaves were burgeoning, and, down on the ground, chickweed, also known as starweed because of its minuscule white flowers, was growing rampantly.

Country people have always used chickweed as a weather barometer (if its blossom shuts tightly rain is imminent), and as an edible winter green, boiled like spinach. Its main value, however, lay in its medicinal qualities. In his *Herbal* of 1653, Nicholas Culpeper called it: 'a fine soft pleasing herb under the dominion of the Moon', and recommended it be used for skin ailments 'of the privy parts' and 'generally all pains in the body that arise from heat'. A pot of beeswax and chickweed salve was often kept by stoves and fires in case of burns and scalds.

Other verdant spots in the otherwise bleak winter garden have always been kindly provided by common groundsel, blooming merrily in the gloom. It has been known since earliest times as a witches' plant (in *Discovering the Folklore of Plants*, Margaret Baker says that this was because the yellow patches of the plant were thought to indicate where witches had urinated); but as it is under the dominion of Venus, it has been long used in home remedies for painful menstruation in young women. In old wives' lore it is also an efficient ingredient in a cream for cracked, 'wintr'y' skin.

In 1952 in her book *Green Medicine*, herbalist Mrs Hilda Leyel was recommending that: 'an infusion of the herb left to cool will remove roughness and whiten the hands.' Its use in sympathetic magic for toothache was recorded in WT Fernie's *Herbal Simples* (1910):

Dig up Groundsel with a tool that has no iron in it, and touch the tooth five times with the plant, then spit thrice after each touch, and the cure will be complete.

Shepherd's purse is often known as 'mother's heart' because of its unusually shaped little seed-pods. This creeping pathside plant, associated with Hecate, starts appearing this month, and was useful in treating cystitis and uterine problems.

Black hellebore, the Christmas rose, used to be known by the name melampode, from a physician called Melampus who supposedly cured the mad daughters of Proteus of Argos with it. As a cure for insanity it was rather dubious, as it is toxic. This eccentric-looking perennial has always been associated with the occult – the Greeks drew a circle round it and chanted prayers before they picked it, and witches, who used it in their 'flying ointment' and 'eternal youth potions', approached it barefooted, head bowed. Country women have used it variously for headache poultices and amulets, to procure abortions, and as a violent purge for intestinal worms. Its Christian mythology is less threatening – Gabriel touched the frozen earth with his staff and created the hellebore so that a poor shepherd girl, Madelon, would have a flower to offer the Christ Child.

During the digging that was part of essential garden work this month, clusters of snails were revealed by the bucketful. Sometimes they were most useful, as this recipe reveals:

Snail Cough Mixture

20 snails from crevices in walls, half a pound moist brown sugar.

Leave snails in a bowl to clean themselves. Remove and place live snails in muslin bag with the sugar. Leave to drip

overnight. Bottle liquid and use a tablespoon as required.
Old Channel Island remedy from *Lotions and Potions*,
National Federation of Women's Institutes, 1968

Ravens were sometimes similarly ill-starred, being used in a
folk recipe to restore black colour to greying hair; and field mice
were utilised in a syrup to cure bedwetting infants. The
mistlethrush, which had sacred associations as it was believed to
feed solely on mistletoe, was regarded with more reverence. Its
call was considered an omen of impending stormy weather.

Jane Loudon's *Practical Instructions in Gardening for Ladies*
(1841) recommended in her 'Calendar of Operations: January'
chapter that women scour their fruit trees for signs of insect
eggs, and that those suspected 'be brushed with soft soap and hot
water'. Mrs Beeton was similarly rigorous, suggesting that at this
time of year sensible females should examine their paper or
muslin bags of seeds for mould, maggots and other such
undesirables. However, if such seed-threatening vermin as rats
or mice were found in sheds, barns or attics, country women
sometimes took the precaution of leaving them this tried-and-
tested charm-note:

> I order all Rattons that be in this house
> All manner of Rattons, and eke of Mouse,
> By the grace of Mary cleane –
> Go hence Rattons! Be ye no more seene!
> *Food in England*, Dorothy Hartley, 1954

The garden was now a happy hunting ground for those with
an arcane turn of mind. Green-lichened lucky ash twigs were
gathered to wear in little silk bags around their necks. Another
choice New Year good luck talisman was a small stone exposed
to moonbeams for three nights running. The first new moon of
the year was particularly fortuitous; the luck-absorbing ritual
involved standing outside with one's eyes shut, while turning
over a bright new silver coin in one's pocket or hand and making

a wish. Housework was not completely forgotten. Heavily stained linen was thought to benefit from the whitening effect of the new moon's rays, and was spread on bushes for lunar purification.

More sensible souls stayed indoors by the fire, reading tarot cards or examining a chart of the solar zodiac – once known as 'Our Lady's Waye'.

January
... as the warm blaze cracks and gleams
The supper reeks in savoury streams
Or kettle simmers merrily
And tinkling cups are set for tea.
The Shepherd's Calendar, John Clare, 1827

February

The great mother of all living creatures, the Earth, is full of seed in her bowels, and any stirring gives them heat of Sunne, and being laid neere day, they grow.

The Country Housewife's Garden, William Lawson, 1617

In February, in the New of the Moon, sow Borage, Coriander, Marjoram, Radish, Rosemary and Sorrel.

The English Hus-wife, Gervase Markham, 1615

> Good morrow, Valentine,
> Please to give me a Valentine;
> I'll be yours if you'll be mine.
> Good morrow, Valentine.
>
> Anon

> Yet mark'd I where the bolt of Cupid fell:
> It fell upon a little western flower,
> Before milk-white, now purple with Love's wound
> And maidens call it Love-in-Idleness.
>
> *A Midsummer Night's Dream*, William Shakespeare

To Make The Body Fat and Comely

Take of Milk and Spring Water each one pint, boyl them together til the water be consumed; then add Sugar of Penedies, fresh Butter, each one ounce, Oyl of Sweet Almonds newly drawn half an Ounce, give them one boyling more, and so let it be taken betimes in a Morning Fasting, and sleep upon it.

The Accomplisht Lady's Delight, Hannah Woolley, in
The Gentlewoman's Companion, 1675

Yet would I be glad to sleep
With golden Aphrodite.

Homer, 700 BC

Mountain gorses, ever golden
Cankered not the whole year long!
Do ye teach us to be strong;
Howsoever pricked and holden.

Elizabeth Barrett Browning, quoted in
The Country Diary of an Edwardian Lady
by Edith Holden, 1906

Of the Leap of the Moon

As the slackness of the sun produces one day and one night always in four years, so the swiftness of the moon throweth out one day and one night from the reckoning of its course every nineteen years, and that day is called *saltus lutae*, that is, the moon's leap, since it overleapeth one day.

Leechdoms, Wortcunning and Starcraft of Early England,
TO Cockayne, 1864

ebruary is named after the Roman goddess Juno Februa – a cleansing, post-winter personification of the goddess Juno. It was a magical month for Celtic peoples, for this was when they celebrated Imbolc – the great festival of Spring Awakening. Brighid, later known as St Bride, patron of midwives, was the great fertility deity of Ireland venerated at the beginning of this month. Effigies of her were made from the previous year's wheat, oats or corn, dressed in woman's garb and sat at the table with the family to enjoy a traditional potato-cake called Boxty before being laid in a highly decorated resting-place called 'Bride's Bed'. Candlemas on 2 February is the Christian festival of the Purification of the Virgin Mary, commemorating Mary's ritual cleansing at the temple and presentation of the infant Jesus to the elders.

Candlemas was said to have been so named because the prophet Simeon called the Christ-child 'a light to lighten the Gentiles'. However, candles/fires/tapers had always been burned in February in shrines to Brighid, and before that as lustration before images of Juno Februa ('the Purifier'), and to illuminate the underworld hunt of Ceres for her daughter Persephone. In Europe for many centuries it was traditional for women to prepare an extra-large batch of rush-lights or beeswax or tallow candles in preparation for Candlemas. 'Lady Candles', or 'Heavenly Candles', were left glowing singly or in great clusters on windowsills at Candlemas.

This was the date by which it was considered imperative to remove all leftover Christmas greenery from the church. Girls went along to their family pews with brooms to remove every last leaf, for to leave even one behind was very ill-omened:

> For look, how many leaves there be
> Neglected there, (Maids trust to me),
> So many goblins you shall see.
>> Robert Herrick, seventeenth century

Known as 'The Whirling Month', because of the often wild, gusty weather, this was also the month of hope, when the first hints of greenery and the first spring flowers started to manifest themselves in the bleak trees and poking through the hard, frozen earth.

Dog's mercury, daisies, winter aconite, winter-flowering jasmine, willow catkins, gorse, alder, cyclamen, violets and primroses were all beginning to appear, along with the first pink tips of peony bushes, whose roots have been carved into amulets and rosaries by country people for many centuries. Dedicated to the moon goddesses Hecate and Diana, whose light they were believed to magically reflect, peonies, like myrtle, were planted very near the house to guard the household against storms. Many of the pioneers of spring were eagerly seized upon for use in the kitchen and stillroom: cyclamens were made into tarts to induce love, and primroses were strewn in a medieval almond and honey porridge, made into handcream and, with gorse buds, used for pre-spring yellow dyes and restorative teas.

Also flowering through the frost was witch-hazel, described by Vita Sackville-West as 'torn ribbons frayed, of yellow and maroon'. This useful plant, beloved by water-diviners, was used to make eye-bathing and anti-bruising decoctions. Lesser celandine, now sprouting uninvited everywhere in most gardens, was a popular ingredient, along with hog's lard and treacle, in salves dealing with 'problems of the fundament'. Mrs Grieve recommends it in a more polite context as featuring along with elder buds and houseleek, in an early spring ointment for abscesses.

The snowdrop, known as 'The Fair Maid of February', 'Mary's taper' or the 'Purification Flower', has always been an emblem of the Virgin Mary. It was used in the Middle Ages for digestive disorders, and a bowl of the blossoms brought into the house would give it 'the white purification' and symbolically cleanse the house of winter ills and lurking malevolence.

The violet, in classical mythology the floral form of the tears of the nymph Io, was used by the Celtic women of antiquity in a beautifying wash. This 'fine plant of Venus', said to represent constancy in love, was beloved by medieval householders as a sweetly aromatic pre-spring strewing herb to replace the rank rushes of winter. The housewife of the past would now be busy making, from early blooms in mild weather, violet sugar, violet vinegar, violet oil that 'assuageth the headache ... and moisteneth the braine', and syrup of violets. She might even be making up Culpeper's colourful remedy for that eternal end-of-winter problem of people who spent lots of time sitting on cold stone benches – aching piles. 'Violets, fried with the yolk of an egg and applied thereto,' was the somewhat abrasive recommendation. More romantically, the subtle, 'secretive' scent of the flower has always been remembered with reverence:

> The smell of violets hidden in the green,
> Pour'd back into my hidden soul and frame,
> The times when I remember to have been
> Joyful and free from blame.
>
> Dream of Fair Women, Alfred, Lord Tennyson

Known as 'love in idleness' or 'heartsease', the vivid-hued pansy, with its heart-shaped leaves, was an essential ingredient in philtres 'for the broken heart', as according to legend Cupid coloured the flower with his arrow. In France it is known as 'Trinity Herb' and has been much used in folk ointments for infants' skin rashes and for soothing cough syrups.

Yellow crocuses were thought in ancient times to be favoured by the gods, who wore crocus-yellow robes. In The Scented Garden, Eleanour Sinclair Rohde (1931) reports: 'The crocus dress of Pallas Athene the Attic maidens embroidered with many colours.'

On certain calendar days, celestial medical assistance was often applied for. St Agatha, an early martyr often grotesquely depicted carrying her bosom around in a dish, was invoked on her saint's day, 5 February, by women suffering from sore breasts and milk-flow problems. An Agatha-amulet made of milk-stone (galactite) was considered a great boon for suckling mothers.

9 February, St Apollonia's Day, celebrated a matronly Alexandrian poet martyr whose torture involved drawn teeth. Her help was much called upon by those who had not found much comfort in homemade dentrifices such as the one recommended by Queen Henrietta Maria, widow of English king Charles I, which included pumice, coral, alabaster and brick dust. An old toothache-prayer to Apollonia begged:

> O Saint Apollonia, by thy passion,
> Obtain for us the remission of sins,
> Which by teeth and mouth we have committed ...

* * *

St Valentine's Day, 14 February, has its origins in the Roman Lupercalia festival honouring Juno and Pan, at which unpartnered young women sought lovers by an early form of lottery. Figs, pomegranates and other multi-seeded fruits symbolising luscious fertility were on the menu in February in the Classical world to conjure Ceres and Persephone from their winter imprisonment underground. There were love divinations galore throughout Europe this month: young German women scattered hemp-seed (a psychoactive aphrodisiac consecrated to Freya, goddess of love) into a bowl of water to see if it formed into a particular initial; while English maids wrote their would-be lovers' names on tiny scraps of paper, rolled them inside little clay balls and threw them into water-basins. The first clay bead to surface represented the destined swain.

In medieval times in courtly circles February was seriously devoted to affairs of the heart. Posies of crocuses, blooming around St Valentine's Day, were given by lovers to each other as an emblem of constancy. According to folklore birds chose their mates this month, so small birds in gilded cages were also considered appropriate love-tokens, along with bird-shaped amulets. So were honeyed gingerbread hearts, heart-shaped love-knot brooches and coloured, decorative sleeves – thus the expression 'she's wearing her heart on her sleeve' and the courtly song:

> Greensleeves was my heart of gold,
> And who but my Lady Greensleeves?
>
> Anon

Elizabethans liked to signify their amatory availability by wearing the ferny green tops of carrots pinned to their clothes and presenting their beloveds with sugary 'Sweetheart Biscuits' which were heavy with dried fruit and flavoured with rose-water.

The well-to-do of this period also had a considerable passion for jewellery. Gentlewomen wore up to a dozen rings at a time, not only on their fingers (and thumbs) but also on chains round their necks and speared to their hats with ornate hat-pins. A love-gift of a ring was thus very welcome, especially if it was engraved with a symbol, initial or motto and featured a jewel like the mystic emerald or the ruby, signifying passionate devotion. Pearl ornaments famously improve their lustre when worn next to the skin. Queen Elizabeth I wore many ropes of them, as well as pearl drops in her ears. In more ancient history, Cleopatra was adorned with Red Sea pearls, symbols of Heaven, at the banquet she gave in honour of Mark Anthony, and the jewel is much associated with their love affair:

> Cleopatra: How goes it with my brave Mark Anthony?
> Alexas: Last thing he did, dear Queen,
>   He kissed – the last of many doubled kisses –
>   The orient pearl.

Ring-giving between lovers as an *aide-mémoire* has been around since ancient times. The Egyptians believed that love flowed directly from the heart to the fourth finger of the left hand, and thus encircled it with emotion-reminders in the form of rings of coloured glass and precious metals. In Shakespeare's *Two Gentlemen of Verona*, Julia gives a ring to Proteus, saying: 'Keep you this remembrance for thy Julia's sake.'

Nervous females who worried that a lusty would-be beau had

slipped a charmed love potion into their drink protected themselves against randy magic by putting an amethyst, identified with fierce Diana the huntress, into their cup. In mythology the virginal nymph Daphne took even more drastic measures against her pursuer, lust-inflamed Apollo. Calling upon Gaia – Mother Earth – for help, she metamorphosed into a laurel tree before her would-be ravisher's eyes. Apollo was so remorseful he made the laurel his sacred emblem.

On Valentine's Day, Elizabethan and Tudor women ate garlic and tomatoes, known then as 'love apples', to provoke unbridled lust in their beaux, or slipped them luscious little purple cakes called 'plum shuttles'. Honey-soaked cardamoms were thought to stimulate alluring-ness, while mussel shellfish, who derive their name apparently from the old English word *mossel*, meaning 'vulva', were devoured in their multitudes by women and men wishing for amatory success. In the seventeenth century, astrologer/physician Nicholas Culpeper advised a rather less blatant close encounter come-on: 'Madeira wine with ginger, cinnamon, rhubarb and vanilla makes a wine with aphrodisiac qualities.'

* * *

Throughout northern and southern Europe in this month people used to make merry with an informal pre-spring carnival before the arrival of the privations of Lent. Among the special food created for the festivities, rural French women made little puff-pastry male and female fertility figurines, while in England on Shrove Tuesday (so called because of the confessions or 'shrivings' people were meant to perform at this time), housewives used up their spare eggs and cooking fat in making pancakes. After midnight lavish food would be frowned on until the end of Lent, so women used rich, densely heavy pancake mixtures bearing little resemblance to the health-conscious puddings of modern times:

To Make Pancakes

Take a pint of cream, and eight eggs, whites and all, a whole nutmeg grated, and a little salt; then melt a pound of rare dish butter, and a little sack; before you fry them, stir it in: it must be made as thick with three spoonfuls of flour, as ordinary batter, and fried with butter in the pan ... strew sugar, garnish with orange, turn it on the backside of a plate.

The Compleat Housewife, Eliza Smith, 1758

Pancakes may be descended from the little moon-shaped wheat cakes ritually eaten at Imbolc – the Celtic festival of spring – in days of old. In Christian times, women traditionally began making the pancakes as soon as the church Shrove bell rang around midday – sometimes a group of them would get together and race to the church in their aprons, flipping pancakes in their frying-pans as they went:

As fit as pancakes for Shrove Tuesday.

All's Well That Ends Well, William Shakespeare

In Ireland the older women sent the young girls off on a farcical treasure hunt for a fictional 'pancake sieve' during the carnival merriment, with an ornamental pancake-griddle as a prize. As well as pancakes, in parts of Britain in this pagan and pious month Bible Cake, or Scripture Cake, was made, using assorted puzzle-clues (these varied from area to area) from the Bible for its ingredients – eg:

half a pound of Jeremiah 6, verse 20 ('sweet cane')
one tablespoon of Samuel 14, verse 25 ('honey')
a pinch of Leviticus 2, verse 13 ('salt') etc, etc

Over the meatless Lenten period fish was an essential part of the menu, often cooked in kettles over the fire, with the addition, for the well-to-do, of oysters, barberries, cloves, mace and nutmeg. Sometimes it was cooked in 'coffins', high-sided pies of raised-crust pastry, with pastry fish embossed on top. Warming spices such as ginger were included, and sometimes, strewings of sugar. Fish, before the advent of Christianity, were the emblems of sea-born Atargatis/Aphrodite/Venus (the same goddess in Syrian, Greek and Roman cultures) whose marine, moon-associated, highly sexual attributes were later translated into the figure of the mermaid in popular imagery. Perhaps because of this association mirrors featured prominently in charms/spells designed to infatuate the idolised one.

After Shrove Tuesday lacemakers, who usually worked together in a group during winter to save money on lighting and heating, would blow out their candles for working by, not to light them again until September. Small presents, such as new colour-ed or clear glass beads for bobbins, would be exchanged among the women. For the female populace at large, housekeeping as well as food management in this last fragment of winter, when stocks in the store-rooms and larder were low or of poor quality, were largely a matter of scrimping and eking out, plus a little borrowing and inventiveness. A fourteenth-century French housekeeping manual called *Le Ménagier de Paris* advised that a good way to get damp wood to burn was to make a tinder from tree-fungus, and that sour, murky wine could be improved with the addition of hot wheat grains and a basketful of Seine sand!

In matters of beautification at this time of year it was pragmatic to use what was to hand: Roman women made do in the winter with a face-mask made of mashed lentils, while Greek women down to their last imported phial made up an 'instant' perfume using vanilla pods, honey and lemon rind. In Greek and Roman mythology the gods left an aromatic scent behind them when they visited humans as evidence of their divinity. It was the job of Juno Nuxia (yet another of Juno's many personifications) to anoint the doorposts of brides with perfume when they first entered their new homes as an auspice of good luck.

However, weddings, along with other merry-making, were generally taboo in later Europe throughout the forty-day pre-Easter Lenten period:

> If you marry in Lent,
> You will live to repent.
>
> Traditional

Sex was also considered an unlucky activity at this time of stringent self-denial, and any children conceived were ill-omened. Concentration on fertility and propagation in garden matters was far more advisable. For as a sixteenth-century gardening writer pointed out, 'the fittest time of the Moone for proyning is when the sap is ready to stirre', and February fits the bill admirably.

* * *

Apart from the pruning of roses, fruit trees and nut trees such as cobnuts and filberts, there was the planting of box, clary sage and hyssop for knot gardens.

> And God said, Behold, I have given you every herb-bearing seed which is upon the face of all the earth.
>
> Genesis

February has always been a time for first seed plantings. Some (eg parsley, marigold, thyme, woad) had to be sown indoors or under glass, but others such as chervil and German chamomile could be scattered directly outdoors. Apart from a few green vegetables such as winter purslane, the housewife's harvest consisted of root vegetables: beets, parsnips, turnips, Jerusalem artichokes all emerged from the frosty soil, along with early radishes. The latter, it seems, have always been useful against Seasonal Affective Disorder:

> For heaviness of the mind, give to eat radish with salt and vinegar; soon the mood will be more gay.
>
> *Leechdoms, Wortcunning and Starcraft of Early England,*
> TO Cockayne, 1864

The same compilation of pre-Norman hints and wrinkles

recommends holly-rind boiled in goats' milk for 'oppression in the breast'.

Various days this month were seen to be propitious for sowing and gathering plants. On 29 February in Victorian times close women friends picked each other early forget-me-nots to be worn in buttonholes. Valentine's Day was a favourite date for setting seeds for peas, lettuce and sweet peas. And, 'On Candlemas Day stick beans in the clay, throw candle and candlestick right away'.

The portent of the weather was watched closely now, for the old folk saying declared:

> If Candlemas Day be fair and bright,
> Winter will have another flight:
> If Candlemas Day it be shower and rain,
> Winter is gone and will not come again.
>
> Traditional

Beehives had to be carefully guarded against severe frosts with straw and old coverlets, for their invaluable occupants 'are tender and nice' said one early writer.

The gusty February weather invariably brought down an avalanche of 'key' seed-pods from the ash trees. A selection of these were gathered and dried to use as protective charms later in the year against all manner of ailments and evils. This old Celtic prayer was an added identification with and entreaty to Mother Earth in a temperamental month:

> I am She
> That is.
> The mother
> Of All Things.
> Mistress, governess
> Of all the elements.

March

In March and in Aprill, from morning to night;
in sowing and setting good huswives delight.
To have in their garden, or some other plot:
to trim up their house and to furnish their pot.
Five Hundredth Pointes of Good Husbandrie,
Thomas Tusser, 1559

March: Wild, Mild and Mothering.
Traditional English saying

As mad as a March hare.

Traditional

Of Hares
She keepeth not her young ones together in one litter,
but layeth them a furlong from one another,
that she may not lose them altogether, if peradventure
men or beasts light upon them.
History of Four-Footed Beasts, Edward Topsell, 1607

I'll to thee a Simnel bring,
'Gainst thou go a-mothering;
So that, when she blesses thee,
Half that blessing thou'lt give me.

Robert Herrick, seventeenth century

Set eggs under hens or other fowls in the new of the moon.

Maison Rustique, C Estienne and J Liebault, 1570,
trans. R Surflet, 1600

To Choose Eggs at Market

Put the large end of the egg to your tongue; if it feels warm it is new. In new-laid eggs, there is a small division of the skin from the shell, which is filled with air, and is perceptible to the eye at the end. On looking through them against the sun or a candle, if fresh, eggs will be pretty clear.

A New System of Domestic Cookery, Maria Rundell, 1807

A March bride will be a frivolous chattermag, and given to quarreling.

The Old Bridal Calendar, England, seventeenth century

nown to the Saxons as Hiyd Monath – 'The Stormy Month' – March officially heralds the season of nature's rebirth after winter. The wild and plaintive calls of the curlew and wild duck above the sound of the grim winds and often driving rain seem to contradict the promising floral and verdant burgeoning in the soil and on the trees. Throughout western Europe this contradiction is echoed in the mixed joy and gloom of the March festivals – because for many centuries the month has been punctuated not only by the fasts and mourning of Lent (named after Lenten-tide month, when the days lengthen), but also by the feasts of Mothering Sunday and Lady Day, the latter celebrating the angelic Annunciation to the Virgin Mary on the subject of her surprising imminent pregnancy.

In March the ancient Egyptians and Hellenes lit candles, baked cakes with horns (in honour of the celestial cow-goddess of nourishment and creation, Hathor) and dedicated flowers, mirrors, exotic perfumes and palm trees to Isis, celestial creator of the universe amd keeper of divine mysteries. The Romans celebrated the beginning of their New Year with the Matronalia, which honoured Juno in her motherly role; and then the Minervalia, offering worship to Minerva, goddess of knowledge, spinning and the moon. At the Vernal (Spring) Equinox around the twenty-first of the month, when days and nights are of equal length, Celtic peoples danced in their sacred groves and lit fires on hilltops to encourage the returning light and warmth.

The women knead their dough, to make cakes to the Queen of Heaven.

Jeremiah

Not only is there traditionally much thanksgiving cake-making this month, it has always been considered the done thing, right back to the days of the spring cleaning of the Vestal fires and putting fresh laurel garlands on the altar, to thoroughly clean out the winter fireplace. In medieval times it was the custom before Easter (which can of course occur in March, as it always falls on the first Sunday after the first full moon of the Spring Equinox) to 'do the fire out of the hall'. This meant not only disposing of the old ashes, but sweeping the hearth, polishing the fire-dogs with flour and salt or rhubarb leaves, and filling the whole area with early, sweetly scented spring flowers and catkin-trimmed branches. The newly shined fire-irons were always stored on the right side of the hearth, as the left was the haunt of malevolent spirits.

Wood ashes were not thrown away, but stored to make lye for washing clothes and household linen (March winds were thought to have magical whitening abilities) and to scatter over the fields and kitchen garden as a fertility charm for newly sown seeds. It was considered most unlucky for the family if a cloud of soot fell down the chimney while the hearth was being cleaned, and the ashes were carefully examined before being swept up for any particularly portentous shapes such as coffins, cradles or wedding rings, which might give a clue to forthcoming events. In rural France the ashes of the last winter fire were smeared on the doorpost in the sign of a cross to protect the house from fire and storms. By Victorian times this early spring hearth decoration still existed, but it had degenerated into extraordinarily fussy fringed fabric tenting:

Ornaments for Grates

Purchase two yards and a half of crinoline muslin, and tear it into small strips ... strip this thread by thread on each side, leaving the four centre threads; this gives about six-and-thirty pieces, fringed on each side, which are tied together at one end, and fastened to the trap of the register [plate], while the threads, unravelled, are spread gracefully about the grate, the lower part of which is filled with paper shavings. This makes a very elegant and very cheap ornament.

The Book of Household Management, Isabella Beeton, 1861

Other household tasks included making the whole house clean and bright for Easter. There was much cleaning of windows with vinegar or cut onions, airing of blankets, scrubbing of floors, and in particular making larders, dairies and all food stores fresh and free from mouldy winter supplies in readiness for the new spring produce. In country areas tasks also included collecting and peeling willow wands for basket-making, and collecting alder shoots for dyeing cloth brown. A major challenge was destroying clouds of emergent fleas by burning brimstone or scattering leaves from the aspen, or shiver-tree, in likely nooks and crannies. It was believed for some time that these invaders came from *outside* the house and had a particular partiality to St David's Day:

If from fleas you would be free
On March the First, let doors and windows closed be.

Traditional English saying

***

Many flowers useful in kitchen and stillroom were beginning to emerge now: primroses and violets (which Shakespeare described as 'sweeter than the lids of Juno's eyes') galore; plus anemones, both pasque (from *Pascha* – Easter) and wind-flowers, dedicated in the language of flowers to all those forsaken by their lovers. In Greek mythology Anemone was a nymph favoured by Zephyr, god of the West Wind, until transformed into a wind-flower by the goddess Flora. Known in Italian as *Fior da Dama* – ladies' flower – anemone has been long used in teas and tinctures for uterine problems, as well as a protective women's amulet:

March wind-flowers so frail and pure
Keep all infection from your door.

Proverb

Lengths of budding periwinkle shoots, once used for Chaucer's 'garlands of Pervenke', were more commonly used in folk medicine for making anti-cramp garters. Ground-ivy – also known as gill-over-the-ground and hedge-maid – clarified and flavoured beer and was a well-known ingredient in anti-ageing bath unguents.

Any early-flowering daisies (from Old English *Day's Eye*) were often plucked, threaded together into a chain and hung inside the house to deflect lightning, the leaves having first been removed to make an anti-bruise salve.

The first young leaves of dandelion were eagerly gathered on the continent of Europe for eating in salads and stews, as well as for making 'dreaming tea'. Witches were reputed to drink extra-strong potencies of this tea to increase their arcane powers, but young women imbibed it for a sneak preview of their futures. The pink and purple columbine was so named because its flower resembles a circlet of doves' heads (*columba* is Latin for 'dove'). Known in Germany as *Akelei*, this strangely formed flower was much used by St Hildegarde as a medicine for swollen glands. In England not only was it thought efficacious for abdominal pains, but it also represented spiritual life, being often used as a symbol in old paintings of the Virgin Mary. It was also thought to be a springtime tonic much devoured by lions!

If March comes in like a lion, it goes out like a lamb,
If it comes in like a lamb, it goes out like a lion.

Old English weather proverb

Whatever the weather, women continued to sow seeds in windowsill pots, and, when possible, in their herb garden. Dill was one of the most essential windowsill herbs, not only for its baby-soothing abilities (in a syrup or tincture), but as a lucky charm that 'hindereth witches at their will'. Gervase Markham's seventeenth-century manual *The English Hus-wife* recommended that 'in March, the Moon being new', it was a good idea to sow garlic, chervil, marjoram, white poppy and marigolds, leaving chicory, fennel, and 'apples of love' (tomatoes) to the full moon. At the new March moon rural English women 'potentised' the holed stones they wore as pendants or hung on the back of the door, by exposing them to the moon's rays. Eye disorders were thought to be much improved by being rubbed with a blue silk handkerchief passed through a wedding-ring by the light of the moon. French women, meanwhile, scattered larkspur seed around the house in moonlight to drive away any lurking ghosts.

The shape of the moon was watched anxiously for weather prognostication at this important seed-sowing time:

> The moon on her back holds rain in her lap.
>
> Proverb

* * *

Cooking in March, with its long period of Lenten denial, was a culinary challenge. Nettle-tops and young tansy leaves, the latter in times past associated with the 'bitter herbs' eaten at the Last Supper, were a popular addition to the diet:

> *Tansy*
> Being qualified with the juices of other fresh Herbs, Spinach, Green Corn, Violet, Primrose-leaves etc at entrance of the Spring and then fried brownish and eaten hot with the Juice of Orange and Suger.
>
> *A Discourse of Sallets*, John Evelyn, 1699

Along the sea-shore women scoured the rocks and strand at low spring tides for the first harvest of seaweeds, which they used as a fertiliser for their gardens, to dry and stuff into pillows and mattresses, and to supplement the family diet. Plump kelps, sugar wrack and Irish moss (also used with salt as an impromptu toothpaste) were taken home to be dried on flat stones or wooden frames. In the Channel Islands and Cornwall some seaweeds were mixed with gin or rubbing alcohol and used as an embrocation.

Bread was often eaten unleavened in the run-up to Easter, and one of these flat 'blessed' Lenten loaves, marked with a cross, was kept all year tied over the stove as a magical aid to help bread rise. Often loaves and rolls were sprinkled with caraway seeds, which not only had powers against evil forces but were thought to be an excellent memory restorative.

The fragrant aroma of more adventurous baking filled the house just before Mothering Sunday, which fell on the fourth Sunday of Lent. This festival probably had its origins in people from outlying churches and chapels visiting their 'Mother' church on this particular holy day, but over time it became a date on which live-in servants were given permission by their employers to go and visit their mothers.

> On Mothering Sunday above all other
> Every child should dine with its mother.
>
> Traditional English saying

This 'Mid-Lent' Sunday was an event on which it was permissible to have a respite from frugality, so girls brought their mothers a rich and heavy (one recipient mistook hers for a foot-stool!) simnel cake, traditionally crowned with violets and primroses, either fresh or candied. Full of dried fruit, lemon peel, almond-paste sugar and eggs, the cake – whose name comes from the Latin for flour, *simila* – has a rock-hard raised crust of flour, water and costly red-gold saffron, whose use among country people was as much a medicinal cure-all as a flavouring and colourant. Sometimes the cakes were made in a star-shape, or sported almond-paste effigies of the Christ and/or the Virgin Mary. Always, however, the cake was embellished with eleven egg-shaped, almond-paste balls representing the apostles, minus Judas.

Figs, universal symbols of ripeness and fecundity, were the main ingredient in a Mothering Sunday recipe for fig pie, which also used almonds as emblems of life, plus spices, eggs and breadcrumbs. Medieval recipes proferred deep-fried fig fingers and fig and almond porridge. In parts of France almond-paste was also eaten on Mothering Sunday, but there it was softened with aromatic flower-waters and formed into large decorative *bon-bons*.

Eggs, the ultimate embodiment of renewal, were naturally used copiously during the Lenten period. As Jane Austen's Emma knew, 'an egg boiled very soft is not unwholesome' – in fact, it is an elegantly simple repast. Roman women prepared their soft-boiled eggs with lovage and pine-kernels, and sometimes a crispy vegetable on the side:

> A Roman meal,
> Such as the mistress of the world once found
> Delicious, when her patriots of high note
> Perhaps by moonlight at their humble doors,
> Under an ancient oak's domestic shade,
> Enjoy'd a spare feast – a radish and an egg.
> > James Thomson, nineteenth century

Eggs – brown, white and speckled – were also used in count-less more imaginative ways. On Palm Sunday (in northern Europe the 'palms' were often made of more readily available spring greenery such as willow, and it was customary to keep the palm cross all year to bring favour and blessing to the house), pax or peace cakes were made. These were triangular puff-pastry shapes representing the Holy Trinity, which included in their ingredients eggs, sugar and apricot conserve.

Other eggy recipes included eggs cooked with leeks, emblem of St David of Wales, whose festival occurs at the beginning of the month; pickled eggs; egg and lemon jelly; egg, saffron and apple tart; baked eggs in saucers; creamy honeyed egg-custards; and of course buttercup-golden omelettes galore, laid on beds of young sorrel or spinach and cheese. Eggs, with their associations of resurrection, were also much utilised in folk medicine at this time of year:

For a Consumption

An approved receipt; by a Lady at Paddington. Take the yolk of a new-laid egg, beat it up well with three large spoonfuls of rosewater; mix it well in half a pint of new milk from the cow ... drink it every morning, fasting for a month, and refrain from spirituous liqueurs of any kind.

The Art of Cookery Made Plain and Easy,
Mrs Hannah Glasse, 1747

There were many complex superstitious household rules and regulations governing the handling of eggs. They were never to be brought into the home, or indeed taken out of it, after sunset, in case they were turned rotten by malovolent spirits. Eggshells had always to be completely crushed before being thrown away so they could not be used as 'magic boats' by those practising the black arts. To dream of eggs meant a forthcoming pregnancy, but to dream of chickens implied betrayal by a loved one or impending financial disaster.

In looking after hens, one had to be careful that there were an uneven number of eggs (ideally 13) set under the mother bird if the eggs were to hatch into chicks, which were thought to be particularly lucky this month. As a proverb puts it: 'A chicken in March is eggs for a year.'

Jane Loudon, in her classic *Loudon's Lady's Country Companion* (1845), advises that chicks should be removed from the hen when hatched from the egg, 'put in a basket on some wool or flannel, and set by the fire'. When all the brood are hatched, she says, they must be returned to their mother and offered boiled rice, boiled barley and a 'few boiled potatoes crumbled small'. Wine-soaked toast was thought to be most encouraging for the mother hen. Those eggs not destined for hatching were stored tightly in a buttered wrapper and straw to keep the air out and ensure freshness.

* * *

Another creature much associated with the month of March is

the hare, which appears as a very mystical animal in many ancient mythologies. Aphrodite is sometimes pictured attended by a hare, and the Saxons worshipped a hare-headed goddess. Hares are elusive lovers of solitude and moonlight and are subject in March, their mating season, to 'mad' leapings. In some European folk legends, rarely seen white hares were believed to be the souls of 'pure girls' who had died of broken hearts, while very dark animals were sometimes thought to be shape-shifting witches, who could only be killed by a silver bullet.

The ancient Romans used to observe the disportings of hares for their divinations, as did the ancient Britons, according to W Hazlitt's 1905 *Dictionary of Faiths and Folklore*:

> A remarkable way of divining related to Bonduca or Boadicea, Queen of the Iceni – when she had harangued her soldiers to spirit them up against the Romans, she opened her bosom and let go a hare, which she had there concealed, that the augurs might thence proceed to divine.

It was believed for some time that these mysterious animals reproduced by laying eggs, a residue perhaps of the story of the sacred moon-hare of Eostre, Saxon dawn-goddess, which was indeed an egg-layer. This may be the origin of the link between the Easter Bunny and Easter Eggs.

The English tradition of eating sweet buns marked with a cross in early spring is a very ancient one. Some sources say that honeyed cakes similarly marked were eaten in the temples of Diana, Roman goddess of the hunt, where the mark divided the cake into quarters representing the seasons of the year. Good Friday hot-cross buns have long been considered to have very special properties. Many families kept one bun all year in the medicine cupboard, where it was grated into a drink as a surefire cure for those suffering from stomach ailments.

Good Friday was a day on which it was thought very ill-starred to do any washing, for fear that Christ's bloodstains would appear on the linen as it hung on the line. Iron utensils, pins, scissors or needles were not touched in some regions because of that metal's association with the naíls of the cross. If a cooking fire needed some attention, it was poked with a stick – preferably a rowan, with its protective, peril-averting qualities. To break any china today of all days did not augur well – but all breakages had to be in threes, according to custom, so two more rough household pieces would be deliberately smashed so that the very best dinner service might be saved.

Conversely, to plant on Good Friday, especially potatoes, was very good luck indeed. Now was also a time to plant another succulent, turnip-like root vegetable – the skirret, hardly eaten at all in Britain now, but used by Eliza Smith in a 'skirret-pye' with cinnamon, nutmeg, chestnuts and eggs in *The Compleat Housewife* (1758). According to *The Art of Gardening* by 'JW' (1677):

> The Skirret, or Skirwort root was also a very ancient dish among the Romans and is the sweetest, whitest and most pleasant of Roots, and by Physicians esteemed a great restorative and good for weak Stomachs, and an effectual friend to Dame Venus.

Parsley, dedicated to Persephone, goddess of the underworld, has always been associated with death and has been hung in tombs since the times of the ancient Greeks. Medieval lore held that a parsley seed had to travel down to the devil (to Hell) nine times before it would grow. On Good Friday, however, the ground was considered to be safe from Satan, and there was a rush to scatter the seed of this most useful herb.

On no account, though, could cuttings be given away or the parsley transplanted, for this boded very ill for giver and receiver alike. Hares, mysteriously, apparently adore parsley. According to Mrs Grieve's *A Modern Herbal* (1931), they will 'come from a great distance to seek it'. Parsley seeds have also been much used in the home apothecary for cures for, variously, ageing, baldness, sore eyes and freckles. Once known as 'woman's salvation', the seeds used to be much employed in homemade elixirs for weeping, windy infants.

April

Ful wel she song the service divyne,
Entuned in hir nose ful semely.

Madame Eglentyne the Prioress in
The Canterbury Tales, Geoffrey Chaucer

Here I heard the first singing of the birds this year, and I here observed an instance of that petticoat government, which, apparently, pervades the whole of animated nature.

William Cobbett

Folk Song
The cuckoo she's a pretty bird,
She rings as she flies,
She brings us good tidings,
She tells us no lies;
She sucketh white flowers
For to make her voice clear,
And the more she sings 'cuckoo',
The summer draws near.

Anon

Candie Flowers

Take your flowers, and spread them abroad on paper, then clarifie sugar ... let it boile ... then put in your flowers ... as soone as they bee through wet in the syrupe take them out, and with a knife spread them abroad on a pie plate, and set them where they may dry.

Elinor Fettiplace's Receipt Book, 1604,
Hilary Spurling (ed.)

April

The weste and northe wyndes ben
good but the south is beste.

The Boke of St Albans, Dame Juliana Berners, 1486

Sit ye my ladies, sink,
Sink ye to earth down;
Never be so wild,
As to the wood to fly.

Saxon bee-charm

It is meet that our hous-wife know that from the eight of the Kalends of the month of April, unto the eight of the Kalends of July, all manner of hearbs and leaves are in that time most in strength and of the greatest vertue to be used and put in all manner of medicines.

The English Hus-wife, Gervase Markham, 1615

Of Rosemary

Take the flowers therof and make powder therof and bind it to thy right arme in a linnen cloath and it shall make thee light and merrie.

Bancke's Herbal, 1525

Hail April, the Medea of the year,
That makest all things young and fresh appear.

The Book of Days, R Chambers, 1866

fter getting up early to see the sun rise on Easter Sunday morning (the sun was reputed to dance to celebrate the Resurrection), devout country women went to church *en masse* to decorate the altar. Flowers and greenery of choice in the country were the arum lily of purity and mourning (the first lily is said to have grown in the tears of Eve as she left Paradise), but wrapped about with glossy branches of yew representing immortality. In the Christian story, the resurrected Christ first appeared at Gethsemane to a woman, Mary Magdalene, who mistook Him for a gardener.

Easter has always been a seasonal turning-point marked by the rebirth of gods and evidence of the renewing divine vegetative energies of spring. The final departure of winter has been celebrated at this time of year in many cultures – in ancient Rome it was symbolised by the reappearance of the goddesses of increase: Flora, Ceres and Venus, who were hallowed by women dancing in sacred groves of myrtle. According to some sources the name April comes from the Greek word *Aphrilis*, or 'of Aphrodite'. Throughout most of Europe April has always been a particularly festive month, for April Fool's Day on the first is descended from the Hilaria, the joyous Roman festival of the Vernal Equinox where people were given licence to behave however they chose.

Easter Sunday has always been honoured with new clothes, or at least new gloves or a new hat – a particularly frivolous 'Easter bonnet' – to celebrate the passing of winter and to attract good luck.

> At Easter let your clothes be new
> Else for sure you will rue.
>
> Old English proverb

This followed on from the custom of wearing the same clothes throughout Lent as an act of penitence. It was widely thought that those who did not make the effort to wear something new would almost certainly be fouled on by passing crows later that day.

Hats, of course, were never worn indoors, for folklore dictated that a headache or incipient baldness would be sure to develop. (Those with a hair-loss problem were advised to pray to St Urban, whose holy day falls on 2 April, and to make a hairwash from radish juice and honey. Another favoured remedy was to make a tonic from the early-blooming flowers on rosemary bushes, and/or to fashion a comb from rosemary wood.)

Most Easter festivities involved eggs – archaic representatives of the universe – in some shape or form. Medieval mothers dyed hard-boiled eggs in cochineal or beetroot and gave them to their children as health-charms (in Greece eggs are still dyed red at Easter). Blown eggs were decorated with ribbons and coloured glass 'jewels' and given as gifts. Children called from house to house on Easter Monday begging hard-boiled eggs known as 'pace eggs' or 'peace eggs', to be used in complex egg-rolling or egg-tapping games. Eggs to be presented within the family were dyed brown with onion-skins, green with anemone and spinach or yellow with gorse. Before they were dyed, a design or a personal name was drawn on with a wax-candle, made with the outline of flowers, petals and delicate ferny leaves, or etched on the dye with a sharp needle or bodkin.

Women hid the eggs all over the house and garden for the children, or, as in Germany, served them up at the table nestling in a plaited wreath or nest of rich glazed bread (decorated blown eggs were also hung by threads on branches as an 'egg-tree'). According to Teutonic legends, eggs were laid on Easter morning only by rabbits. French children were given not only sweet edible almond-paste eggs but also homemade chocolate fish, which were both a reference to Christianity and a passing nod to April Fool's Day, known in France as *Poissons d'Avril* ('April Fish'). Fragments of eggshells always had to be protected against imagined evil spirits and sorcerors who might use them in a spell – but on Easter morning in many parts of Britain it was propitious to throw them into a holy well along with a bent pin or a holed stone to be sure of the achievement of spring wishes.

With so many eggs in demand the lady of the house had to keep her eye on how many primroses she brought into the house. For although primrose was considered to be a lucky flower – once much devoured by small children desirous of seeing fairies – an old wives' tale held that the number of primroses in a bunch determined the number of eggs successfully hatched by the hens. No fewer than 13 flowers were thus ever allowed in a primrose posy.

Crisp little round, sugary Easter-cakes, tied in bundles with red ribbon – and, according to Alison Uttley's *Recipes from an Old Farmhouse* (1966) 'with a little bunch of flowers' on top – were exchanged by English women friends on Easter Sunday. Sometimes they were cooked on sycamore leaves and bore the imprint of the leaf. In Italy the favoured pudding on this day was the *Columba di Pasqua* – an elaborate white cake made in the shape of a dove, the classic representation of the Holy Spirit, and the bird of Venus. It has always been traditional for French women to make almond-paste, puff-pastry and crystallised fruit Easter cakes in the shape of a large fish.

* * *

Nettles, with tender shoots, to cleanse the blood!
 Cry of the herb-women, London, eighteenth century

The bounty of blossom and verdancy in the hedgerows and garden now had the household manager's full attention, for as much as possible had to be cooked for everyday use or pickled, candied, macerated or distilled for storage. Young nettles were picked and eaten as a medicinal salad or as a pot-herb with barley and the pink spikes of the bistort herb in Easter savoury 'Passion Puddings' and stews. In 1661 Samuel Pepys sampled some:

To Mr Symon's where we found him abroad, but she, like a good lady, within, and here we did eat some nettle porridge.

Hildegarde of Bingen recommended young, fresh nettles to 'purify the stomach' and 'rid it of excess mucus or phlegm', while later lady home-herbalists garnered the new crop on behalf of 'Dame Physic' as a remedy for gout, rheumatism and menopausal problems. Nettles were also used to tightly wrap spring cheese; Gervase Markham prissily observed in *The English Hus-wife* that so-wrapped, 'the fewer wrinkles that your cheese hath, the more dainty is your Housewife accounted.'

Elder buds, young bracken fronds, wood sorrel (under the astrological sign of Venus, and a Celtic sacred plant), and hawthorn buds were eaten as a snack, and the buds of marsh-marigold (dedicated to the Virgin Mary) were pickled. New borage leaves were lightly cooked in fritter batter or made into tea to cleanse the blood. Trefoil-leafed red clover, a symbol of the Holy Trinity, fertility and general good luck to women, was always grown near the house to delicately flavour spring cheese, attract benevolent fairies and make a soothing unguent to rub into split and cracked post-winter nails.

Syrup of pansies was made to guard against 'sadness respecting domestic affairs', and juicy new dandelion leaves – legendarily the favoured wild nourishment of Hecate – were harvested both for salad and to make potent beer and wine (traditionally made in England on St George's Day, 23 April). Naturally, given their symbolic importance, eggs were thought most potent now for medicinal use. In M Woodward's *The Mistress of Stanton's Farm* (1939) the redoubtable Grandma Stanton recommended a treatment for a spring cold made out of new-laid eggs kept in a jar with lemon juice for nine days. It was advised that the home-apothecary 'remove the blue mouldy top' and add rum and sugar-candy in great quantities.

In April, churches and houses were strewn with fresh rushes and scented iris leaves after a top-to-toe cleaning and polishing:

Sweep your house, who doth not so,
Mab will pinch her by the toe.
                    Robert Herrick, seventeenth century

Mugwort or anemone was worn pinned to women's clothes as a talisman against tiredness during these vigorous travails. Hildegarde in the twelfth century recommended spiritual fumigation of the house in spring with oak leaves, geranium, marshmallow and broom. According to folklore, witches gathered spring growth of cinquefoil for potions and to burn aromatically near the cauldron while they incanted their spells. Most other women gathered it at the wane of the moon to make medicines to counter fevers, painful menstruation and gum diseases, as well as to hang over the front door as a charm against supernatural forces.

The clear bright fire, the whitened hearth, the yellow-ochred walls, the polished tins, the clean-scrubbed tables and chairs, and the white dresser-cloths, of the kitchen, such as I have always been used to see at my own house.
                    The English Housekeeper, Ann Cobbett, 1851

When the hearth was given its spring-cleaning and the fire extinguished (the exact date depended on the weather), wooden painted 'dummy-boards' of people and/or animals were sometimes stood nearby to 'guard' the hearth in the absence of its usual attendants. Sometimes it was made to look even more like a shrine, as described in this seventeenth-century extract from *The Queen-Like Closet, or Rich Cabinet*, written by Hannah Woolley:

To dress up a Chimney very fine for the Summertime as I have done many, and they have been liked very well
Take ... Moss ... of several sorts of kinds, and place here and there carelessly ...; then any kind of fine Snail-shels, in which the Snails are dead, and little Toad-stools, which are very old

and look like Velvet, or any other thing that is old and pretty; place it here and there as your fancy serves, and fasten all with Wax and Roisin. Then for the Hearth of your Chimney, you may lay some Orpan-Sprigs in order all over, and it will grow as it lies; and according to the Season, get what flowers you can, and stick it in as if they grew, and a few sprigs of Sweet-Bryer. A Chimney thus done will grace a Room exceedingly.

This was the time of year when the few 'bought' essentials of the kitchen, store-room and stillroom were replenished, the most important of all, for preserving, being salt. The ancient Greeks believed that salt was not only sacred and the essence of life itself, but was also an emblem of true friendship. This veneration and the superstitions attached to it have lasted through the ages – until this century country women carried tiny bags of 'purifying' salt in their pockets to attract good fortune. If any were spilled it was to be either tossed over the left shoulder to appease the devil, or into the flames of a fire (perhaps an echo of the days when salt was burned on the altars of the Greeks). According to ritual, when the table is laid for a meal the salt must always be the first thing to go on to it and the last thing to be removed. An old saying, 'Help to salt, help to sorrow', signifies that this condiment is not something to be passed around casually.

* * *

With the advent of the balmier weather, great spring washing sessions were undertaken. It was generally thought inadvisable to wash the new clothes of Easter when there was a full moon, or the fabric was sure not to last well.

If the washing were undertaken indoors, it was a rule that the water had to be thrown out before nightfall. Trampling the clothes in the clear, fresh water of a spring stream was highly desirable. A crisply upstanding effect on collars and cuffs was achieved in country households of the Elizabethan era by making starch out of bluebells and arum lilies. It was an old adage that 'April showers make May flowers', but that was no comfort when washing-day loomed. The housewife wanted to know on what Shakespeare called 'the uncertain glory of an April day' whether or not to hang out her garments and linen to dry. Canny women looked to see if the sow was squealing and scuttling, fleas biting, spiderwebs broken, black beetles marching about the kitchen, the bees keeping to the hive and the hens huddling, which all meant that bad, thundery weather was imminent. If that wasn't enough, there was also a storehouse of helpful weather-sayings to guide the would-be laundress:

> If it rains before seven,
> It will be dry before eleven.

* * *

As well as grafting and pruning in the orchard, the women of the household had to busy themselves with the care and observation of the beehives, for the young bees were getting ready to swarm out of their overcrowded home, and this was a good time to collect new young honeycombs for the manufacture of the very best beeswax candles, furniture polish and special healing ointments.

It was advisable for the novice apiarist to carry a sachet of the 'blessed herb' herb bennet to prevent 'the biting of venomous beasts', and to keep her mouth firmly closed, for it was commonly thought that swallowing a bee would prevent a woman from ever conceiving a child. In parts of Germany and Austria hives were hand-painted with stars and moons and hung with an amulet of the Virgin Mary – 'Mother of the bees', so called because bees have been sacred since ancient Egypt. In William Lawson's early seventeenth-century English classic, *The Husbandry of Bees, Published With Secrets Very Necessary For Every Housewife*, the reader is advised to protect her bees from 'showres and rubbish' and ideally fashion for them a delightful new conical house:

Comely made of Fir boards, to sing and sit, and feed upon your flowers and sprouts, make a pleasant noyse and sight. For cleanly and innocent Bees, of all other things, love, and become, and thrive in an Orchard.

It was said that where daffodils (Lent lilies) grew unplanted and wild in a garden there was once a medieval monastery or nunnery on the site, for those in the religious life were partial to the sunny flower and planted it about their cloisters and enclosed gardens. Dedicated to Persephone, the daffodil, 'in her yellow petticoat and her green gown', was once used as a purging tonic and its roots boiled in oil for use in an emollient unguent for heels chafed from heavy winter boots and shoes.

> Daffodillies yellow
> Daffodillies gay
> To put upon the table
> On Easter Day.
>
> Old English saying

The other useful golden flower flourishing this month was the early cowslip, once dedicated to Venus and to Freya, the Norse goddess of sexuality and the holder of the Keys of Paradise. It has always been thought to have fairy associations:

> In their gold coats spots you see;
> These be rubies, fairy favours;
> In those freckles lie their savours.
>
> A Midsummer Night's Dream,
> William Shakespeare

The plant was highly valued for its piquant edible qualities. M Woodward's 1939 The Mistress of Stanton's Farm advises that the flowers be mixed with sixteen eggs, three pints of cream, rosewater, sugar and sweet biscuits to make a cowslip pudding. It also possessed seemingly magical cosmetic properties, indeed so much so that Nicholas Culpeper remarked in his 1653 Herbal:

Our city dames know well enough the ointment or distilled

water of it adds to beauty or at least restores it when it is lost. An ointment being made with them taketh away spots and wrinkles of the skin.

Another potion to leave the skin 'fresh, fair and lovely' was made from a distillation of Solomon's Seal, also known as St Mary's Seal. The similar-looking lily-of-the-valley or lady's tears – the flower of Ostara, Norse goddess of springtime – was thought useful to comfort 'the vital spirits' and 'settle the brain of frantic persons', as well as to restore fading memories.

* * *

The garden also offered augury through bird-song. The cuckoo was thought to be a fairy bird who knew both where treasure was hidden and the identity of one's true love. She was also the symbol of summer, appearing only when the seven-starred constellation of the Pleiades (the doves of Venus) materialised in the sky, and to hear her haunting notes was to know that winter was truly over:

> Summer is icumen in,
> Lhude sing cuccu!
> English thirteenth-century song, Anon

14 April was officially known as First Cuckoo Day. When the first cuckoo cry was heard, it was good for future fortunes and future crops to take off the shoe of the left foot and at the same time to turn over any silver coins in pocket and purse. A cuckoo feather was a powerful charm against the evil eye. It was legend in some areas that the birds were let out of a mysterious old wisewoman's basket on the 14th, having slept underground all winter. This story perhaps descends from Greek mythology, in which the cuckoo was one of the many emblems of Hera and was borne on her sceptre.

To hear the cuckoo cry at night, however, especially during the dark of the moon, was generally thought to be lamentable. To hear it on St Mark's Eve, 24 April, was especially alarming, for this was a night when the wraiths of all those destined to die in the next year were meant to troop around the churchyard. Brave souls sat in the church porch for three nights in a row to check if their *doppelgänger* were part of this alarming spectral vision.

Sensible folk stayed at home, taking advantage of the occult nature of the night to do some useful divining. This was done by sifting the ashes of the fire, or, if the fireplace had already been cleared and cleaned, by spilling beans or chaff on the hearthstone. If at midnight a footprint mysteriously appeared there, this belonged to the future lover of someone in the room. But alas, if the footprint was pointing towards the door the portent was supposedly more sinister, hinting at an untimely demise for one of the participants. Luckily, as this was still the topsy-turvy month of jocularity and rejoicing, people didn't take these otherworldly signals too seriously, especially if the spiced cherry beer was flowing freely.

St Mark's Eve was considered a very good night for fruitful dreaming, especially if a bag of dried vervain or primrose leaves was tied to each of the bedposts, a moonstone worn in a bag around the neck, and a mirror placed under the pillow. To dream of eggs, the theme of this month, was to predict the manufacture of something important and creative: the conception of a child or success in an undertaking, or (if the eggshell was broken) a quarrel with a friend.

Those very keen to find out the identity of their future lover would do some alarming midnight laundry, for as the old saying goes:

> On St Mark's Eve at twelve o'clock,
> The fair maid will wash her smock,
> To find her husband in the dark,
> By praying unto good Saint Mark.

It was all to the good for eligible women if Mr Right did *not* materialise, however, for an *Old Bridal Calendar* solemnly informs us: 'An April bride is inconstant, not over-wise, and only fairly good-looking.'

A Spring Gargle for the Throat
Red rose buds dry and unfolded about a tablespoon, to which
add half a pint of boiling water. After letting it stand an hour,
strain and add a tablespoon of rose vinegar and a little sugar
if you like.

> *The Housekeeping Book of the Saunders Family Women,*
> Ann Saunders

The fair maid who the first of May,
Goes to the fields the break of day,
And washes in dew from the hawthorn tree,
Will ever handsome be.

> Ancient proverb

A Cosmetic Water
Wash the face with tears that issue from the vine during the
months of May and June.

> *The Toilet of Flora*, PJ Buchoz, 1784

A choir of bright beauties in spring did appear,
To choose a May-lady to govern the year.

> *Lady's Song*, John Dryden

Button to chin, till May be in.
Cast not a clout, till May be out.

Ancient proverb

Who would live for age
Must eat sage in May.

Proverb

Nettles have other economic uses besides making thread. The juice of Nettles prevents wooden tubs from leaking; it coagulates and fills up the interstices. Nettles make good fodder for cows, and the seeds mixed with food given to poultry to increase the hens' laying power. The seeds are also an ingredient of hair tonics.

Herbal Delights, Mrs CF Leyel, 1937

ush with visible signs of the earth's renewed fertility, May has been associated since primordial times with vegetative magic and the Great Mother via her various incarnations: the Sumerian Lady of the Evening and the Morning Star Inanna; Maia and Flora, Roman goddesses of growth, increase, plants and flowers; Scandinavian Maj, the virgin goddess of spring; Gwynhyfar or Guinevere, the May Queen of the earthly paradise of Joyous Gard; and the Virgin Mary. May was known of old as the 'Merry Month' or 'Honeymoon' because of the ritual promiscuity that took place at this time throughout Europe, not only in pagan days but right until the advent of the puritanical ethos in the seventeenth century. Back in ancient Rome Aspasia recommended that women protect themselves during the revels with contraceptive herbal tampons made of wool.

Unsurprisingly, this has long been the month associated with blossoming womanhood. In ancient Greece girls who had reached puberty were expected to give their dolls up on the altar of Aphrodite, goddess of erotic love. *Parthenoi* virgins went through an initiation rite that involved a girls' camp at Brauron where girls dressed as she-bears and ate figs and snake-shaped 'wise' biscuits.

> Bore at seven, the mystic casket;
> Was at ten, our Lady's miller;
> Then the yellow Brauron bear;
> Next (a maiden tall and stately with a string of
> figs to wear)
> Bore in pomp the holy Basket.
>> The Women's Chorus from *Lysistrata*,
>> Aristophanes

Girls in ancient Rome were often given a Menstruation Feast by their mothers to welcome them into the community of women. This featured red fruits like pomegranates and cherries, and gifts like moonstones and a set of sea-sponges for the bleeding. In Scandinavia and the Highlands and Islands of Scotland mothers took their daughters aside and showed them the menarche kit of sphagnum moss sanitary towels and boiled dandelion root or flax cramp curative.

Throughout Britain mothers recommended for their daughters daisy-sap for pimples, and for pain chamomile stomach poultices and tea or soup from pennyroyal and mugwort. The latter, commonly known as 'Muggins', was (and still is) used throughout Europe by herbalists as a uterine cycle regulator under the astrological Dominion of Venus. Its botanical name, *Artemisia*, honours the contradictory deity Artemis, virgin hunter goddess of both unmarried girls and women in childbirth – whose other incarnation is the Great She-Bear Ursa Major, guardian of the stars.

> If they wad drink nettles in March
> And eat Muggins in May,
> Sae mony braw young maidens
> Wad na' be gang to clay.
>
> Scottish proverb

For many centuries young girls wishing to know what the future held in store for them slept on a pillow to which five (considered a 'woman's' number) bay-leaves had been affixed, one in each corner and one in the centre. The divinatory bay would conjure an oracular dream featuring the girl's future spouse. There may have been a considerable element of disappointment in the morning! Usefully, Elizabethan physician John Gerard recommends in his 1597 *Herbal* a disappointment decoction of marjoram, 'as it easeth such as are given to much sighing'.

* * *

Imminent summer is traditionally heralded by the Celtic fertility festival of Beltane, celebrated at night between 30 April and 1 May with vast hilltop bonfires, a vestigial reminder of fire-offerings to Celtic lunar deity Brigit and her forerunner, the Phoenician moon-goddess Tanit. This night, known as Walpurgis in central Europe and Valborg in Scandinavia, has always had sinister overtones, for it has always been a powerful witches' Sabbat.

> When I see the new moon,
> It becomes me to lift mine eye,
> It becomes me to bend my knee,
> It becomes me to bow my head.
>
> Celtic prayer collected by
> F Marian MacNeil, *The Silver Bough*,
> William MacClelland, 1956

In England, according to popular legend, this was the night when witches made new broomsticks of ash and birch and daubed themselves with flying ointment (an hallucinogenic salve of aconite, heliotrope, spurge, maidenhair, belladonna and henbane) while chanting flying formulae. Women fearful of bad magic would protect their babies from being substituted with elfin changelings by putting salted crusts tied with red thread in their cradles or fastening red coral amulets round their necks and/or wrists.

Thresholds could be guarded from evil with a barrier of holed stones known as 'hag-stones', the flowers of the marsh-marigold ('Herb of Beltane'), and leaves of angelica, a mystical plant believed to be of heavenly origin. Protective trees of elder, named after Hulda, Norse fertility icon, were planted outside houses, stables and byres to keep dangerous witchcraft at bay.

* * *

Mayday celebrations (known in France as *Les Jeux Floreaux*) have always been associated with the gathering of greenery from the hedgerows before sunrise. 'Going a-Maying', a direct descendant of the cult of Flora, traditionally meant gathering birch, rowan and, best of all, swathes of white blossom from the hawthorn or 'May', long a tree of healing, divination and blessing, with which to decorate the doorway of the house. 'Bringing Home the May' was usually a women-only celebration accompanied by much singing of the traditional chant 'Here we go gathering knots of May ... ' Sometimes women and girls left torn strips from their dresses and aprons on the bush to ask the vegetative spirit of the Hawthorn or the Virgin Mary for a blessing.

On this day women often wore green dresses, or clothes decked with green ribbons. At any other time it was considered unlucky, as green was deemed the chosen hue of the fairies *and* an insult to the green of nature. Girls also used garlands of hawthorn to deck the Maypole, usually a young tree brought in from the forest. Latterly, the pole-tree has been interpreted as a crude phallic fertility symbol, but some academics think the tree and its intricately interlaced ribbons are vestiges of a complex Assyrian lunar calendar.

> Sister awake! Make haste, I say,
> And let us, without staying,
> All in our gowns of green so gay
> Into the Park a-Maying!
>
> Anon

The highlight of Mayday was the choosing and garlanding of the May Queen, a comely maiden who had no doubt washed her face in the May-dew: a highly desirable cosmetic ritual thought to keep ageing at bay. Elizabeth I always had May-dew brought to her first thing on 1 May, and Mrs Pepys and her maid scuttled out at 4am of a May-morning to look for some droplets. The best dew was said to be found beneath oaks, or on ivy or alchemilla leaves, and a secret wish was imperative during the ritual wash.

In ancient Roman times May was also the time of the 'secret' women's festival known as *Bona Dea* – 'The Good Goddess'. It is thought that the deity honoured was Vesta, the hearth guardian. Roman matrons and Vestal Virgin priestesses gathered together in spiritual sisterhood at the home of one of the group, burned sacred herbs in a brazier, swept the room with a vervain broom (vervain is sacred to Venus), and made merry in house and garden with food and drink. Men were absolutely forbidden; even their statues were covered. Plutarch records that Cicero had to go and stay with friends while his wife and her friends celebrated *Bona Dea*.

> But far off we heard the laughter of cloistered maids ... a hut shone with sweet fires of incense.
>
> Propertius IV, ix, 23

Rosemary was burned by the Vestals as a fragrant offering during the funerary festival of Lemuralia, which occurred in May. Since then it has been a 'women's herb', much favoured in medicines for 'women's ailments' as well as in flavouring food and storing clothes aromatically. In many countries a few sprigs of the blooming herb were cast on a spring fire for good luck and remembrance of times past; also bunches of it were used to brush and scent wooden floors for special occasions.

* * *

A sense of sisterhood and female camaraderie was essential in the days when every woman was her family's household manager, gardener, cook, pharmacologist and physician. With the late spring garden burgeoning with useful culinary, household and medicinal plants for stews and simples, and a huge harvest to come in the ripe summer months, it was essential on top of everyday chores to cleanse containers and bottles in the stillroom and pantry, and dry early herbs and flowers on hanging racks and (for delicate flower-heads) custom-built airing trays in a dark, dry corner.

It was common practice for women to help each other with these tasks, for the workload was enormous and the botany involved in picking and sowing seeds and plants at the astrologically correct time highly complex. It was deemed essential to plant under the most auspicious zodiac sign (May's plants are mainly under the dominion of Venus) and to sow seed during a waxing moon. Venetian *emigré* Christine de Pisan, in her fifteenth-century treatise *The Treasure of the City of Ladies*, advised French women of the court that tending the herb garden was essential in a well-run, holy household.

A garden enclosed is my sister, my spouse ...

The Song of Solomon

Outside in the garden there were sweet violets, angelica, cowslips (known as our lady's keys) and primroses to collect for crystallising with egg-white and sugar. A fine goose-feather was often used for application. Pickled primroses were prescribed for 'the phrensy' and those in need of dreaming. Late cowslips were made into a love-divination charm called a 'Tisty-Tosty' and drunk macerated in wine for headache, hysteria and loss of memory.

Three or four handfuls of cowslip flowers, cast into a bath very hot, take away tiredness.

Mrs Harrington's Book, eighteenth century

In the sixteenth, seventeenth and eighteenth centuries in parts of Britain, bluebells were used for glue and for stiffening muslin collars. Children, however, were rarely sent to the woods to pick them for fear of abduction by fairies lurking near this 'fairy flower'. Celandine was not only used for wart cures and whitening teeth – it was also a visionary herb once used by witches to clean their glass scrying balls. Women with sore nipples or swollen lactating breasts made soothing 'bra cups' from frilly alchemilla ('lady's mantle') leaves. Nicknamed 'woman's best friend', alchemilla – from the Arab *alkemelych* or alchemy – was sacred in the Middle Ages to the Virgin Mary and was often laid as an offering on stone 'altars' in the countryside by women wanting her intercession on some matter. Leaves from May sage plants were made into a tea to prevent miscarriage.

Periwinkle ('sorcerer's violet') was an essential ingredient in poultices for skin complaints in England and in aphrodisiac philtres in Hungary. At the end of May elderflowers were used for wine, complexion tonics and insect repellent, but women were always careful never to break any elder branches in collecting them – for this would bring bad luck from the Elder Mother and her wood nymphs. For the same reason women would never allow anything made from elder-wood into the house or permit it to be burned on the fire. Respect for elder (known in Scandinavia as Lady Ellhorn) was also based on the fact that it, along with rowan, has always been used to make witches' wands.

This was the month to divide up large houseleeks into smaller cuttings and plant them on the roof to keep lightning from striking, to make up a protective personal amulet of peony root, betony and artemisia wrapped in a tiny red cloth bag, and to construct a fairy-blessed besom from the broom bush (but only after it had finished flowering, or bad luck would ensue).

Dandelions, associated with Hecate and the Celtic goddess Brigit, were used in salads and for beer- and wine-making. Star-flowered woodruff was harvested for scenting books and linen. Throughout Europe (especially Germany), sweet cicely (also known as anise-chervil) – sacred to the Virgin Mary and St Cecilia was planted, as its seeds were made into a beeswax paste for polishing and perfuming special wooden furniture. Myrtle (used widely in cooking and as a love-token) was planted with special care – it always had to be planted by a woman, who had to observe a ritual of spreading her skirts over it to 'hide it' as she placed it in the earth. In Greek mythology Myrrha, favourite priestess of Aphrodite, was turned into this scented evergreen bush to escape an unwelcome suitor. It was always planted around Aphrodite's temples.

For those unfortunates who had no garden, itinerant 'herb-women', or 'simplers', would call carrying vast baskets on their heads of every useful herb for simples or salads, plus apothecaries' powders and nostrums of their own devising.

* * *

As little laundry as possible was done in this 'merry month', but when it was, clothes were dried if possible on flowering rosemary bushes. This was partly for aromatic purposes and partly for reasons of myth and folk magic. In early Christian lore it was said the herb was blessed with blue flowers because the Madonna hung her cloak on it during the flight into Egypt.

Where rosemary grows, the woman rules.

Ancient English proverb

It was considered unlucky to wash blankets in May, for you will 'wash your love away'.

Elizabethan women picked cuckoo-pint in May to make into root-starch for their ruffs and cuffs. If two women had their hands in the same starching basin, however, it was common for one of the pair to spit in the water to avert shared misfortune. The domestic alchemy of stain-removal – sorrel for this, vinegar for that – was lore passed down from mother to daughter and shared between friends. There was a strong oral tradition in domestic lore among women who could not read or write.

* * *

Bees were of prime importance in May, for it was the time when they swarmed with the queen and could be 'claimed' by anyone whose land they alighted upon. Women made new hives attractive to passing swarms by rubbing the insides of the skeps with thyme or lemon balm, whose botanical name *Melissa* means 'honey'. This herb was sacred to the Temple of Diana, and bees – widely thought of until the nineteenth century as creatures of mystery and prediction – and their honey have always been linked to the cult of the Great Mother. It was traditional to talk to bees – to tell them of family news and troubles.

* * *

Inside the house was a hive of special culinary activity. On May mornings Scottish country women made Beltane bannocks:

simple flat pancakes of barley, oatmeal and water shaped like the full moon. These were considered even more magical if cooked over a 'need-fire' flame taken from the Beltane blaze. In Greece, women still make honeyed moon-cakes and leave them on their doorsteps in honour of Artemis/Mary, Queen of Heaven, as they have done for hundreds of generations.

Mayday foods reflect the fact that May is the month in which the cow's flow of milk is meant to be at its best and most rich: custards, cheesecakes, syllabubs, caudles, junkets and 'hasty puddings' were all 'sacred' fare, often decorated and flavoured with primroses, violets and lemon balm, with a spoonful or two buried in the garden as a libation to nature. In May pastry was often decorated with charms of dough plaits and hearts to reflect the love interest of the month and 'make it light'. Yeast for brewing and baking was often marked with a heart and/or a cross to prevent the fairies from stopping it working.

On Mayday milkmaids danced around their houses and those of friends wearing garlands of spoons and other silvery objects to bring the moon's good luck for the rest of the year. If the weather was warm during their frivolities they kept their milk 'cool' in the pantry with sprinklings of mint stirred with a hazel stick:

> Mints put into milk,
> it neyther suffreth the same to curde,
> nor to come thick, insomuch that
> it layed in curded milke, this
> would bring the same thinne againe.
> *The Good Huswife's Handmaid*, Anon, 1597

Homemade sugar confections known as sugar plate were twisted into Maypole spirals and coloured with May flowers. In *Elinor Fettiplace's Receipt Book*, dated 1604, the Oxfordshire-born author describes dyeing sugar plate: 'with the juice of Violets colour a piece blew, then with the colour of Cowslops colour another piece yellowe'.

May was traditionally a difficult month for cleaning the house because of the prevalence of spiders. These industrious spinners have always been identified with women because of their association with mythical heroines like Penelope, Ariadne and Arachne as well as the goddess Athene. The three Fates or *Moerae* of ancient Greece were individually responsible for spinning the thread of life, winding it and cutting it short. It has been considered very unlucky in many cultures to kill a spider or destroy its carefully constructed web, which is a symbol of the cosmos. 'Who kills a spider, bad luck betides her' is a well-known English country saying. In folk medicine deserted webs were commonly used on cuts to quickly stop bleeding.

Nettles were collected in May to make into nettle-fibre for spinning. Many spinning wheels had 'lucky' naturally holed stones as spindle-whorls to protect the cloth from malign influence.

* * *

As this was a month of strong magic, in some rural areas country women would chalk a 'witch baffler' or complicated protective pattern on the front doorstep, representing the spider's 'web of life'. At the least they would carry out a cleansing ritual of whitening the threshold step with a soft rubbing stone known as a hearth-stone, in honour of the white boughs of hawthorn blossom over the door. In humble homes, women would often also decorate their stone or earthen floors with ornate decorative floor-patterns of pipeclay, red ochre or dock-leaf juice. These patterns varied not only from area to area (in parts of Scotland, Wales and the north of England), but also between families – as the designs, often featuring circles and loops, were passed down matrilineally. And sometimes the hearth, like the doorstep, would be whitened in honour of the new 'need-fire' from the Beltane blaze.

Among peasant women it was customary to leave a gift of rich May milk for Hob, the hearth-goblin, last thing at night. In Germany and Scandinavia similar rituals were observed for home-sprites called Heinzlin and Nissen.

One of the taboos linked to the Temple of Vesta is the forbidding of any hair- or nail-cutting until the Ides of June. This may be the origin of the old belief that it is unlucky to cut hair or nails in May – it was widely believed that witches would be lurking about to collect the fallen hair and parings for unsympathetic magic. To catch any malevolent influence that might descend the chimney, hearths sometimes incorporated a 'magic' rowan-wood post, and were often hung about with bottles filled with red threads, and glass rolling pins containing protective salt.

* * *

Cats and hearths and women are inextricably linked in myth and history. The cat, as an object of worship, was in its golden age around 3000 BC when the Egyptian cat-headed goddess Bast, the cosier incarnation of Hathor the fierce lioness deity, was in her heyday. The Teutonic goddess Freya was partial to careering about in a chariot drawn by cats. Medieval witch-terror cast cats in a very bad light as familiars of 'witches', and thus the devil, a fear which was possibly at its zenith in the seventeenth century. Then it was firmly believed by zealous churchmen and their followers that May-born kittens were particularly ill-favoured by their association with this magic month, and should be drowned.

> There is in some men a natural dislike and abhorring of cats; their natures being so composed, that not only when they see them, but being near them and unseen (and hid of purpose) such men fall into passions, frettings and sweatings, pulling off their hats and tembling fearfully.
> *History of Four-footed Beasts*, Edward Topsell, 1607

June

The young maid stole through the cottage door,
And blushed as she sought the plant of power:
'Thou silver glow-worm, oh lend me thy light,
I must gather the mystic St John's wort tonight.'

Old German poem, Anon

Old garden rose trees hedged it in:
Bedroft with roses waxen white,
Well satisfied with dew and light,
And careless to be seen.

Elizabeth Barrett Browning

O! then I see Queen Mab hath been with you.
She is the fairies' midwife, and she comes
In shape no bigger than an agate-stone
On the forefinger of an alderman,
Drawn with a team of little atomies
Athwart men's noses as they lie asleep.

Romeo and Juliet, William Shakespeare

The fairy land buys not the child of me.
His mother was a votaress of my order:

And in the spiced Indian air, by night,
Full often hath she gossip'd by my side.
>   Titania in A *Midsummer Night's Dream*,
>   William Shakespeare

Du Lait á Madame
Boil a quart of new milk, and let it cool sufficiently to allow
the cream to be taken off; then rinse an earthen jar well in
every part with buttermilk, and while the boiled milk is still
rather warm, pour it in and add the cream gently on the top.
Let it remain twenty-four hours, turn it into a deep dish, mix
it with powdered sugar, and it will be ready to serve. This
preparation is much eaten abroad during the summer.
>   *Modern Cookery for Private Families*, Eliza Acton, 1845

Song
O Love! that stronger art than wine,
Pleasing delusion, witchery divine.
>   Aphra Behn, seventeenth century

And let them also bring in hand,
Another gay girland
For my fayre love of lillyes and of roses,
Bound truelove wize with a blew silk riband.
>   *Epithalmion*, Edmund Spenser, 1595

his often hot and heady midsummer month takes its name from Juno, the multi-faceted Roman moon-mother goddess with her origins in early antiquity. Both a home-defensive warrior and a peaceful patron of household and family, she was honoured at the *Vestalia*, where processions of women went to her temple and the sacred Vestal hearth to ask blessing and protection for their households with gifts of peacock feathers, cowrie shells and lotus flowers.

Also fêted were Minerva, goddess of wisdom, whose statue was draped in a new saffron mantle embroidered by high-born matrons wearing white veils; and Fortuna, goddess of fate, who was caroused by people picnicking in small boats on the Tiber. In ancient Greece, this was the month of the *Skirophorion*, when the mother-goddess of Athens, Athene, was worshipped at the Parthenon with a festival where young girls twirled parasols, sun-emblems, in her honour. Earlier still, in Mesopotamia, the cult of Inanna/Ishtar/Isis climaxed with a midsummer rite of epic proportions.

The English pagan month of Rose Moon has as its highlight, as everywhere else in the northern hemisphere, the summer solstice ceremony to give the sun extra power during the winter. The longest day of the year has always been celebrated by a chain of fertility-invoking clifftop bonfires, a custom which still continues in Cornwall. Sickle-shaped floral tributes were cast into the flames to the 'Lady of the Flowers', and herbal amulets were hung on standing stones. It was common throughout rural Europe for sweethearts to leap hand-in-hand over the embers. All household fires were extinguished in honour of the midsummer blaze.

Christians tried to channel popular enthusiasm for Midsummer Eve and Midsummer Day (23/24 June) into the concurrent Feast of the Nativity of St John the Baptist, but many of the old beliefs and customs continued unabated. Midsummer Eve was believed to be a night of exceptionally strong magic – country women made their homes spick and span so as not to offend the fussy fairy folk. They also gathered herbs believed to have supernatural powers such as orpine, St John's wort (a sun symbol), mugwort, dwarf elder, ivy, yarrow, corn marigold and plantain to garland over the door with a green ribbon to keep any unpleasant otherworldly manifestations from crossing the threshold.

Midsummer Eve was the night young women made imitation 'Mandrake' and 'Womandrake' puppets from briony roots and put them on their windowsills to be 'activated' by moonlight and turned into lucky sexual talismans. It was also common throughout Europe for young women to put yarrow (the name comes from *hieros*, 'sacred', as this Venus-ruled plant was often used in women's ceremonies in ancient times) under their pillows as a 'dreaming herb' to conjure visions of their true loves. Sometimes yarrow-filled black pincushions stuck with pins spelling the woman's name were hung on the bedpost. The ancient Egyptians believed that dreams were fortune-telling messages from the goddess Isis.

> Thou pretty herb of Venus' tree,
> Thy true name it is Yarrow;
> Now who my bosom friend must be,
> Pray tell thou me tomorrow.
>
> *Popular Rhymes*, Halliwell

Love potions of vervain, once sacred to Aphrodite and Venus and used by Druids as a herb of prophecy, were covertly made and sometimes covertly administered by being slipped into the person's drink or food. If the favoured one responded amorously, secret recipes for contraceptive tea made from Solomon's seal (known as the Seal of the Blessed Virgin in medieval times) were available. If trysting in the dark, young people carried minute, hard-to-see fern seeds in their pocket to promote invisibility.

* * *

Being sacred to Juno, protector of the household and childbirth, the month of June was thought highly favourable for weddings in Roman times, and the tradition has lingered. The usually prearranged family liaisons of yesteryear were often politically and/or financially advantageous to the *paterfamilias*, who had no truck with weeping adolescent wenches in love with the wrong person. For some 2000 years dismayed brides-to-be have been comforted with soothing chamomile tea or a love-sickness/ jilting philtre of cyclamen.

Preparations for the wedding, and indeed the ceremony itself, were steeped in magic. In their marriage-chests, or 'bride-wains', many girls in medieval Britain kept lucky lace-making bobbins carved from bones from successful past wedding feasts they'd attended. The normal contents of such a dowry-box were exquisitely embroidered clothes and sheets, but in early medieval Scandinavia brides were allowed a shield and an axe in case their husbands became violent! The wedding expression 'tying the knot' dates back to Babylonian times, when threads taken from the garments of bride and groom were ceremonially woven together. 'Hen nights' on the wedding eve are widespread. In rural Germany young women gathered at the bride's new home for the *Polterabend*, where a merry, tipsy racket was made with pots and pans to scare ghosts away, while in Sweden friends went to the bath-house for a nude drinking and gossiping session.

On the day, brides and bridesmaids alike wore veils to confuse the evil eye, and sometimes held small mirrors in their hand for the same reason. The English bride carried a sprig of gilded rosemary, the herb of remembrance, which was traditionally cut for her from the bush outside her mother's front door. On reaching her own new home, the bride would ceremonially plant her sprig – keeping up the continuum for her own daughters-to-be.

Young French women wore homemade combs of mystic rosemary wood in their hair and German women hid tiny caskets on their person containing a pearl, emblem of the moon and the 'chaste Diana'. In the Scottish isles, brides were given talismanic heirloom amber necklaces called 'lammer beads' by their mothers the night before the wedding.

The bride dress could be any colour but green, which mocked Mother Nature and invited an early burial. The 'something old' was usually also the 'something borrowed' – the wedding veil handed down from mother to daughter. Sky blue, favoured in myth by Venus and the Virgin Mary has always been used in amulets against ill-health – many women wore a 'something blue' bead around their neck from cradle to grave. An alternative was a blue ribbon adorned with the shells of snails, long associated with healing. Myrtle, sacred to Aphrodite, was worn as a chaplet in the hair. It was the duty of the chief bridesmaid to plant a sprig of the myrtle beside the bride's rosemary at her new home. To her fell also the symbolic last stitch on the bride's dress, to be completed on departing for the church, and the carrying of the bride-cake, made by the bride's female friends and sometimes shaped like a wheatsheaf, emblem of fertility.

A sensible country bride always informed those divine messengers, the family bees, of her marriage, whilst still in her bridal regalia, and left a piece of cake and a celebratory mug of beer by the hive for them to ensure her future good luck and fertility. It was also deemed fortuitous for her to feed the cat before leaving her old home.

Before the advent of paper confetti, well-wishers rained cereal grains and nuts on the newlyweds to ensure their fecundity, the origin of the sugared almonds in evidence at every Italian nuptial. Even early this century farmers often asked brides to bless their crops to ensure a bountiful harvest, residual vestiges of the cult of Ceres/Demeter.

In *Romeo and Juliet*, Shakespeare has Lady Capulet call for 'quinces in the pastry' – referring to the fruit's sacred role at marriage feasts. Believed to be the original 'apple' which the biblical Eve offered Adam, the quince was the chosen fruit of Venus on Mount Olympus.

The origin of the word 'bridal' is the lucky bride-ale which many girls brewed to sell on their wedding day at inflated prices to friends and neighbours in order to raise money for their new household.

It was considered very bad luck for the new bride to touch the dangerous threshold on her entrance into her new home – thus the custom of being carried (or in Scotland tossed!) over the doorstep into the room. Boiling water was poured over the threshold just before she arrived as a precautionary measure.

The first ritual in medieval times was for the new wife to appease the household gods. If the house was new-built, one of her shoes would already have been placed under a flagstone in the floor as a good luck offering – this personal talisman, always associated with a person's life essence, represented the blood sacrifice of yore. Lore demanded that the new householder brought with her a box of salt, a loaf and a new broom (Romany brides are not considered married until they have jumped over a broom). Mother-in-law, as the outgoing clan-mother, stood waiting by the hearth to present her with her regalia of office as new mistress of the hearth – a pair of fire-tongs and a poker.

In Roman times the nuptial bedroom was lit by sacred hawthorn brands, while in England in Shakespearean times the mother-of-the-bride, no doubt an ardent amateur astrologer and cosmologist, checked that the wedding bed was placed in a fortuitous east-west direction – the path of the sun – and that the special nuptial quilt was embroidered with good-luck runes and the star signs of the betrothed.

Crackly dried verbena and valerian leaves – believed to be powerful aphrodisiacs – filled the pillows, relaxing marjoram was strewn on the floor, and an amorous punch was made up from passion-inducing carnations and pinks. In some parts of Europe women wishing to repel the advances of their betrothed and/or avoid conception wore amulets of poppyseed and walnuts and slipped a sleep-philtre of dill, opium poppy, hemlock or honeysuckle into his loving cup.

Once established in her household, a young rural woman wealthy enough to have access to a stillroom would discover that June, of all the months, enabled her to create a personal paradise in and from her garden. The ancient Greeks thought that souls in heaven drifted about on carpets of flowers – and the housewife with her busy summer harvest in herb-garden and potager was close to this spiritual ideal. She gathered sweet-smelling rushes and grasses to strew on the floor. Herbs and flowers being now at their most aromatic, she collected in bulk for drying, powdering, infusing, distilling and concocting – allies from nature for the long, difficult winter months ahead.

* * *

Thick growing thyme, and roses wet with dew
Are sacred to the sisterhood divine.

Anon

Thyme has always been a powerful women's herb. Tradition, claims Maud Grieve in her 1931 A *Modern Herbal*, claims wild thyme as one of the plants chosen to make the bed of the Virgin Mary. Greek maidens wore it in their hair to make them irresistible to their lovers. Medieval women made little cushions of it to wear under their headdresses, so its balsamic fragrance could ward off melancholia, and embroidered bees hovering over sprigs of thyme as a favourite motif. Apart from its culinary associations with poultry, eggs and cheese it has traditionally been gathered to treat nightmares, coughs and worms in children, and stored with linen to keep moths at bay.

Vita Sackville-West once wrote in a poem that the rose was 'not English as we fondly think'. The rose's origins were probably in Asia, but the flower was especially sacred to the Greeks and Romans, whose mythology linked it with Eos the goddess of dawn and with Venus/Aphrodite. One legend describes how the goddess Flora, having found her favourite and most beautiful nymph lying dead, called upon all the other Olympian gods to help transform the body into the most beautiful flower of all time. Rose petals were scattered from on high at secretive ceremonies known as 'mysteries', honouring the cult of Venus –

the origins of the expression 'sub rosa' for any secret happenings, and indeed of the ornamental 'ceiling rose' in domestic architecture.

In Herrick's poem about Sappho roses were white until they tried to rival her alabaster complexion, whereupon some of them blushed for shame. For Christians, the red rose represents the Virgin Mother, and the flower's five petals the secrets of the confessional.

In the Middle Ages the rose was not only a mystical flower but also a symbol of courtly love and a pudendum emblem. In Chaucer's *Romaunt of the Rose* women languidly wandered in flowery meads and summer pavilions entwined with heavy blooms.

Medieval women in fact utilised the garden, and roses in particular, in a very practical way. They used homemade rose-water in cooking as well as in washing and scenting their clothes. It was also customary to welcome dusty travellers with a bowl of rose-water. These practices continued into the nineteenth century, as did the making of aromatic rosary beads from rose-petals. French country women still swear by rose vinegar to anoint the temples when they have a migraine or are *desolée*.

The petals from heavy, blowsy midsummer roses were never wasted, but garnered day by day and preserved in deep dishes with salt. Often they were mixed with orris root, cloves and other fixatives and put in 'Sweet Bagges' to fill the nostrils of anyone opening a storage box on a winter's day with the captured scent of summer. Young women kept a rose picked on Midsummer Eve by their beds for a month. If the flower retained its shape and colour they could be sure their lover was faithful.

* * *

Some say that lavender water was invented by St Hildegarde of Bingen in the twelfth century. Certainly the 30 species of the botanical genus *Lavender*, which begin flowering in June, have always been associated with mysticism, meditation and all things womanly. Along with rosemary, lavender has been burned as incense since time immemorial. In the seventeenth century, herbalist John Gerard said the plant was not only good for perfuming apparel and gloves, but also for all 'griefes and paines of the head and braine', and for those that 'swoune much'. Elizabeth I partook of endless restorative goblets of lavender water for her famous migraines, and like the rest of her court attempted to clean her decayed teeth with a paste of lavender and charcoal.

The smell of lavender, dried bunches of which were hung on the bedrail and in the cupboard.

Colette

Roman women not only used lavender (from the Latin *lavare* – 'to wash') as a pungent bathing herb, they also repelled bedbugs and moths with lavender sprigs attached to the mattress. The volatile essential oils in this herb had the double purpose of attracting healthy sleep and restful dreams, for the Romans greatly feared the negative Underworld elements of the dark. This *angst* no doubt stems from the complex mythology of the Greeks, who personified night as the star-spangled goddess Nyx, mother not only of Hypnos (Sleep), but also Moros (Doom) and Thanatos (Death). Perhaps this is the origin of the old European folk belief that inhaling the scent of lavender at night enables one to see ghosts.

> Lavender, sweet blooming Lavender
> Six bunches a penny today.
> Lavender, sweet blooming Lavender,
> Ladies, buy it while you may.
> Just put one bundle to your nose,
> What rose can this excel?
> Throw it among your finest clothes,
> And grateful they will smell.
>
> Old London street cry

* * *

96

During this usually hot summer month country women would have so much garnering to do in their own gardens, apart from helping with the hay-making and sheep-clipping, that cartwheel sun-hats draped with lavender were popular to allay giddiness. Some older Cotswold country women still make a protective cream from buttercups and Vaseline, or a sun-soother from the magical elderflower, called Lady Ellhorn's salve. In Saxon times, waterlily juice was considered to give both skin and psychic protection at the height of the sun's powers (a practice dating back to the yonic beliefs of ancient Egypt, where lotus petals represented the sacred pudendum of Isis), and babies and small children were given a rub down with magically protective breast-milk before going outside on a hot day.

Elder flowers featured also in this cooling sunburn recipe:

> If your face be troubled with heat, take Elder flowers, Plaintain, White Daisy root and Herb Robert, and put these into running water, and wash your face therewith at night and in the morning.
>
> *The Gentlewoman's Companion*, Hannah Woolley, 1675

Those hoping to see fairies put clover-leaves in their shoes while they worked outside. The hives of the family bees – believed in ancient days to be the souls of Aphrodite's priestesses, *melissae* – were moved near hyssop and lime flowers, also beloved by butterflies.

It has always been thought a wrongful and unlucky act to damage or kill a butterfly, for in folk culture they have been associated with human souls, especially those of stillborns, and those babies who had died before they could be baptised. Women who had lost such infants often left small dishes of honey in the garden to feed the tiny fluttering spirits in limbo.

* * *

One of the most serious, and lingering, taboos in the kitchen garden was smelling the bean flowers. Since Roman times, beans have been associated with death and rebirth, and it was thought that smelling their flowers brought on prophetic dreams of an unpleasant nature. Bean pods, however, were a popular wart cure; they were rubbed against the offending extrusion and then buried beneath an ash tree.

In the kitchen, drifts of fragrant rose petals were made into rose honey, rose-water jelly sweets, rose-petal preserve, rose butter and syrups of roses, while wild clove pinks (maiden pinks) – also known as dianthus, 'Flower of the Gods' – were transformed into pink marmalade or spicy tea. Peasant women powdered calendula petals, used medicinally for the 'tremblings of the heart', to make ersatz saffron, the holy golden colour of the sun, for cooking and as a hair dye. Big round cheeses were often coloured with it, and on Midsummer Eve these cheeses were rolled down hills to mimic the setting of the golden orb. Floral 'sallets' (salads) were consumed, followed by 'cold junkettings' (custards) dusted with finely sieved loaf-sugar and mortar-pounded violets.

Luscious seasonal fruits such as strawberries and cherries were used in vast pies with complex pastry designs of lattices, crescents, lozenges and mazes – sacred domestic geometry whose pleasing symmetry represented the order of the universe. In coastal areas of Britain 'fairy loaves', in reality sea-urchin fossils, were collected from the beach in the summer and placed by the hearth as symbols of plenty against a hard winter.

Swathes of 'holy' hyssop, or glass 'walking sticks' filled with white beans, were affixed over the door lintel to repel robbers. (Hyssop, with its strong, distinctive aroma, was also used in many parts of Europe as a prayer-book marker, to prevent dozing during church services.)

* * *

With a sudden change in the summer weather presaging a ruined harvest or a comfortable winter, women were on the look out for prognostication omens. Unwarranted loud creaking of furniture was a popular weather lore standby, as were black beetles and ants running across the floor.

Star- and moon-wishing were best done on a clear June night, although it was thought to be disrespectful either to point at the stars or to gaze directly at the moon. A thin handkerchief usually served as an impromptu veil for the supplicant, and turning round three times was thought to add to the magic of the occasion.

> Starlight, star bright,
> First star I see tonight,
> I wish I may, I wish I might,
> Have the wish I wish tonight.
>
> Mother Goose nursery rhyme

* * *

Protecting the family linen and other precious treasures against mice and invading insects was problematical at this time of year. Poor women had to make do with baskets woven from the stems of periwinkle (sorcerer's violet) and strong-smelling herbs, such as aniseed and southernwood, to deter pests. The better-off used aromatic wood chests – particularly favoured were imported coffers made of the red, scented cypress tree, once worshipped as a goddess in Cyprus, which bears her name.

> In cypress chests my arras counterpoints,
> Costly apparel, tents and canopies,
> Fine linen, Turkey cushions boss'd with pearl,
> Valance of Venice, gold in needle-work,
> Pewter and brass, and all things that belong
> To house, or housekeeping.
>
> *The Taming of the Shrew*, William Shakespeare

July

The glorious goddess clothed her as she lay
With beauty of the skies, her lovely face
With such ambrosial unguent first she bathed.
                    Penelope visited by Pallas, *Odyssey*, Homer

Of small houndes hadde she that she fedde
With rosted flessh, or milk and wastel bredde.
                    The Prioress, *Canterbury Tales*,
                    Geoffrey Chaucer (1387)

            The Star
        Twinkle, twinkle, little star.
        How I wonder what you are!
        Up above the world so high,
        Like a diamond in the sky!

                    song by Jane Taylor,
                    early nineteenth century

And at our gates are all manner of pleasant fruits, new and
old, which I have laid up for thee, O my beloved.
                    The Song of Solomon

Summer Sage Cheese

Sometimes the green curd is pressed into a tin or wooden mould, so as to form a dolphin or some other fanciful figure ... or one portion of the milk is coloured red with the juice of boiled beet-root, another green with the juice from spinach leaves flavoured with sage, and another yellow with the bruised petals of the marigold.

Loudon's Lady's Country Companion, Jane Loudon, 1845

On Saturday night I lost my wife,
And where do you think I found her?
Up in the moon, singing a tune,
And all the stars around her.

Mother Goose nursey rhyme

Fairy folks are in old oaks.

Traditional English saying

his sultry month of late haymaking, the midsummer moon and sudden summer storms is associated with an assortment of festivals for unlikely saints and the mysterious 'dog days', when Sirius/Canicula the Dog-Star rises with the sun, symbol of golden goddess Demeter. In what is often the warmest month in the northern hemisphere, there was a pattern in women's culture throughout Britain from early times of 'well-dressing', propitiating the spirits of 'holy' wells with pictures (often of biblical scenes) made of mosses and brightly coloured flower-petals pressed into damp clay. Worship of luck-bringing divining and healing pools continued into Victorian times in the form of the suburbanised 'wishing well'.

The unusual female entities celebrated in the Christian pantheon this month include St Mary Magdalen, patron of penitents and prostitutes – though at no time in the gospels is she described as the latter; some believe she was actually the wife of Jesus. They also include the homely but enigmatic St Anne, mother of the Virgin Mary, patron of housewives and venerated in secret rites by the Knights Templar (a religious fighting order during the medieval Crusades) as Anna Perenna, mother of the Aeons. Another is St Wilgefortis, also known as Uncumber, who legendarily sprouted an immense beard overnight in a bid to rid herself of suitors chosen by her father.

* * *

In these humid, thundery dog days, household hounds were often dosed with syrups made from the wild dog-rose in a bid to prevent them from getting rabies, and the galls on these thorny briars made by the gall-wasp were made into a powder to treat the rest of the household's summer stomach ailments. The tiny white flowers of eyebright were garnered in July to infuse to make eye lotions. The official name of this eye-herb is Euphrasia, from Euphrosyne, one of the Three Graces and a handmaid of Aphrodite. Flies were kept off children by washing them with a homemade insect repellent of elderflower water, and by tying onto their sunhats bunches of mint (under the astrological dominion of Venus, and named after the nymph Minthe). Mosquito and gnat bites were treated with ivy juice (ivy was a holy plant in ancient Greek, Roman, Druidic and Christian traditions) or the sap of the magic 'storm protector', houseleek – believed to affect the weather and to be a universal curative.

Until early this century it was a common practice in various parts of Europe to cure small children of a wide range of summer maladies such as persistent stomach upsets by passing them through a holed stone or a specially split ash sapling. (Ash is the sacred universal tree of Yggdrasil in Norse Edda mythology and is generally revered as a representative of nature.)

Strawberries were believed to be the fruit of Venus, the Virgin Mary and the Scandinavian/Teutonic goddess Frigg (who sent dead babies to heaven in a strawberry carriage), and were recommended in bulk in Victorian times to revive anaemic young girls. Those with irregular periods and menstrual cramps could rely on the delicious ancient remedies of rose-petal tea and rose-petal sandwiches. However, for country women whose gynaecological problems resulted from dalliance in the hay-bales, stronger herbal folk remedies were brought into play. As Flora Thompson relates in *Lark Rise to Candleford*, written in 1939: 'the women had a private use for pennyroyal [to procure abortions], though judging from appearances, it was not very effective.'

In Sweden, women made much home physic from the flowers of the linden, traditionally said to house many friendly domestic sprites. In England, July remedies included tansy flowers worn in shoes as a charm against fever. Vervain (known as the holy herb) – gathered when the Dog-Star was in the sky – and a decoction of the sacred thistle, *Carduus benedictus* (said by Beatrice in Shakespeare's *Much Ado About Nothing* to be 'the only thing for a qualm'), were universal cure-alls.

* * *

The stone-slabbed dairy, stillroom and larder were cool places to seek sanctuary on these hot, oppressive days – dim, quiet places where whey dripped and juices seeped from endless muslin-covered bowls full of rosy, luscious summer fruits like red currants, cherries, strawberries, and loganberries. Creamy white meadowsweet was made into jellies 'for the delectation of littel maids', freshly gathered lavender blooms and cornhusks were used for 'thunder tea' to relieve tension headaches and to make into sugared lavender conserve for soothing 'the panting and passion of the heart', as John Gerard's *Herbal* puts it.

The virtues of lavender were promoted by the medieval Welsh physicians of Myddvai, who claimed to have received their herbal knowledge direct from the mysterious Lady of the Lake of Arthurian legend. Sunburn, they advised, was best soothed by lavender vinegar. Bunches of starry feverfew hung in festoons in the stillroom, for as Gerard says:

> Venus commends this herb, and hath commended it to succour sisters ... and to be a general strengthener of their wombs. And if any grumble because they cannot get the herb in Winter, tell them, if they please, they make a syrup of it in summer.

Girls sat in the welcome chill of the dairy churning rich July butter from cows fed on sweet clover and wildflowers, singing the guaranteed butter charm:

> Come butter come, come butter come,
> St Peter stands at Heaven's gate,
> Waiting for a buttered cake,
> So come, butter, come.

> Traditional song

This was the month when seeds were harvested from the flowering canopies in the garden for household use or further plant propagation – appropriate in a month associated with Persephone, Queen of the Underworld. The symbol of this daughter of the corn harvest goddess Demeter is a pomegranate bursting with seeds, representing the fertility of the earth during Persephone's annual visit to her mother. Elizabethan and Tudor country women often gave departing guests either little pots of basil, whose heart-shaped leaves symbolised love and good fortune, or little material bags and sachets of freshly gathered flower seeds. Kitchen garden and flower garden seeds were also swapped by women farmers when they went to market (if they had to walk long distances they put revitalising magic mugwort in their shoes). As Thomas Tusser said in his quaint but bluntly sexist sixteenth-century treatise, *Five Hundredth Pointes of Good Husbandrie*:

> Good huswives in Somer will save their own seedes,
> Against the next year, as occasion needes,
> One seede for another, to make an exhange,
> With fellowlie neighbourhood seemeth not strange.

Medieval, Elizabethan, Tudor and Jacobean gentlewomen wandered in their leisure time through mysterious low-level mazes and parterres of aromatic hyssop, lavender and box, gathering inspiration for their complex embroideries and tapestries. Their early Victorian counterparts entertained themselves gathering nosegays of blossom to give to friends of both sexes, for the language of flower symbolism had been introduced to England in the early eighteenth century by Lady Mary Wortley Montague from the Muslim harem world of Constantinople, where imprisoned, constantly chaperoned women used flowers as a complex, secret, coded language. The first flower dictionary – *La Langue des Fleurs*, written by Madame Charlotte de la Tour – appeared in France as early as 1818 to guide the uninitiated in the esoteric meanings of such flowers as globe amaranth (which betokens immortality) and honeysuckle (which ensures generous and devoted affection). Throughout the Georgian and Victorian periods these dictionaries were extremely popular with women, who used them to express forbidden passions.

Playing on the grass among the hum of the midsummer insects while their mothers worked, small children (in the peasant class, only very little children were allowed leisure) made daisy chains but were warned to avoid foxgloves. These were not only poisonous but were thought to be 'fairy thimbles' which should not be picked to avoid the wrath of the little folk. Rings of early-morning toadstools or inedible mushrooms were also to be avoided in case of fairy enchantment – and mothers admonished children never to sleep in the shade of the elder tree or 'eld' for the same reason. In July, hazel trees were coppiced, not only for broom-handles and dowsing rods, but also – as they were considered to be magical trees – to make 'fairy-traps' to dot around the garden. Here's a seventeenth-century recipe from an Ashmolean Museum manuscript quoted in Dorothy Jacob's 1964 book *A Witch's Guide to Gardening*:

To Enable One to See Fairies

A pint of sallet oyle [salad oil] put into a vial glasse; first wash it with Rose water and Marygolde water: the flowers to be gathered towards the east. Warm it till the oyle becomes white, then put it in the glass, and put thereto the budds of Hollyhocke, the flowers of Marygolde, the flowers of wild Thyme, the budds of young Hazle, and the Thyme must be gathered near the side of a hill where the fairies used to be: and take the grass of a fairy throne then all these put into the oyle in the glasse and sette it to dissolve for three days in the sunne and then keep it for thy use.

With such a cornucopia of fruit burgeoning on every tree and bush (glass wind-chimes kept the birds away), a succulent few could be spared for beautification. *The Good Huswife's Handmaid* of 1597 (Anon) recommended a mask made of strawberries, tansy herb and milk. Strawberry juice was also used as an efficacious tooth-cleanser. Plums and cherries and 'apricocks' were mashed into a paste to be used on blotchy and irritated skin. Even cherry stones were not wasted, as this old prognostication rhyme – also applied to magpies – demonstrates:

> One for sorrow, two for joy
> Three for a girl, and four for a boy.
> Five for silver, six for gold
> Seven for a secret never to be told.

Country girls recovered from the rigours of the hot summer day (if they were lucky) with a quick splash of well water or a frolic in a stream, but the well-to-do are advised in Sir Hugh Platt's *Delightes for Ladies* of 1605 that a wholesome homemade steam-bath should be made, which should be covered 'with a sheet of your pleasure', not only for modesty's sake but 'lest any sudden cold should happen to offend you whilst your body is made open and porous to the ayre'.

In the privacy of such a tented *baignoire*, blond hair was enhanced with concoctions of hollyhock, mullein and rhubarb; red with marigold, radish and privet; and dark with sage and rosemary. Cheeks were burnished rosy with rough lily pads and abrasive pondweed.

Women living in coastal villages went to the beach for discreet rock-pool bathing and to harvest seaweed for fertiliser, medicine, food, and as a weather barometer: at the approach of rain seaweed becomes moist. They also collected large, flat stones for clothes-smoothing, and shellfish, whose disused carapaces were used for decorating the garden.

The children's nursery rhyme 'Mary, Mary, Quite Contrary', which mentions a garden filled with cockle shells, refers not only to the ancient habit of lining seaside garden pathways with shells and homemade grottoes, but also to the Elizabethan anti-Catholic campaign. The Mary referred to is Mary Queen of

Scots, and the 'garden' is the Catholic Church. The 'cockle' is vernacular for the French *coquille* – the scallop shell symbol of St James (St Jacques) the fisherman, whose festival falls on 25 July, and a symbol worn in the hats of Catholic pilgrims before the Reformation. The 'pretty maids all in a row' may well represent Catholic nuns from Mary's native France. In those days young women in religious orders were invariably from well-to-do families and were allowed to look reasonably fashionable!

* * *

Fishermen are legendarily superstitious, and even early this century in Shetland they were reported to 'still buy winds in the shape of knotted handkerchiefs or threads from old women who claim to rule the storms'.

One of the most obsessional terrors of sea-going men used to be mermaids. Mermaids are direct descendants of the sirens – the singing bird-women of ancient Greece – and of the Semitic moon-goddess known variously in Syrian/Greek/Roman cultures as Atargatis/Aphrodite/Venus. Traditionally they carry as their emblems a mirror and a comb. The former is not in fact a symbol of vanity but of the goddess' astrological planet (now known as Venus), and her comb represents her prolific fertility. Cornish beachcombing women kept smooth sea-glass that they found as fertility amulets, calling them 'mermaids' mirror-bits'. The scallop-shell that decorates seaside gardens is also a symbol of mermaid sexuality.

Rural people in particular lived in awe of thunderstorms in the past, not only because of the apparent otherworldly nature of the phenomenon, but because they frequently ruined all-important crops. Women in country districts of Germany and Austria practised a storm-calming ritual which involved opening a window and throwing out a handful of corn or barley with a shout of 'Take it! It's yours! Now stop!' In many parts of Europe it was considered wise for women to cover mirrors during a storm 'to deflect the lightning', and to open all the doors and windows to allow the thunder to pass through the house without obstruction. Protective amulets made of a fragment of previously storm-blasted tree, or acorns from the Druidic oak tree, were frequently worn.

> No tempest, good July,
> Lest the corn look ruely.
>
> Weather proverb

In drought conditions, the household cat used to be watched most carefully, for it was believed that if a cat spent an especially long time washing its face, the longed-for rain was imminent. July rain was often described as 'Mary Magdalene washing her handkerchief'.

* * *

Feeding the fruit trees in the orchard was one of this month's jobs – it was not uncommon for old shoes and hair trimmings to be used to supply minerals and nutrients. In England it was traditional for apples not to be gathered until after 15 July – the feast day of the Saxon 'weather saint' Swithin, traditionally associated with rainy weather. After this date 'blessed' fallen fruit was gathered for jam, apple marmalade (a sort of apple butter), sweet apple curd and chutney-making:

> Till Swithun's Day be past,
> The apples be not fit to taste.
>
> Proverb

In Holland, women gathered the first tart July windfalls to make sweetsour apple breakfast bread. Apples are associated not only with Eve's fruit of knowledge, but in earlier times with Hera's magic apple garden of the Hesperides, Pomona the Etruscan apple-mother and the Celtic Avalon ('Apple Isle') of Guinevere. Apples are still used in the Midlands of England in a traditional July dish called 'Heg Peg Dump'. 'Heg' was an old country name for hedgerows, where the other ingredients, such as wild plums or damsons, grew. 'Peg' was the familiar name for

Margaret, a medieval dragon-fighter and patron saint of childbirth whose feast day was 20 July. 'Dump' is an English West Country name for dumpling.

The bounty of July flowers that were gathered for eating included the sunflower, whose buds were boiled like artichokes, nasturtium flowers and leaves, buttercup buds, hollyhock leaves and passionflower blooms. In France, catmint flowers (thought good for preventing nightmares) were sprinkled on salad. Marigolds were said in Hannah Woolley's *The Gentlewoman's Companion* to be 'good for melancholly'. Throughout Europe roses, like many other summer flowers, were preserved by candying for autumn and winter use as sweetmeats and decoration.

Preserving Whole Roses, Gilliflowers or Marygolds
You must first pick the seeds out before they do shed. Then dip the flower in syrup consisting of Sugar Candy boiled, then open the leaves one by one with a smooth bodkin of bone or wood, and as soon as they are dipped lay them between two dishes upon papers over a very gentle Fire: and so you may keep them all the year.
Fairfax Household Book, seventeenth/eighteenth centuries

There have always been those of course who prefer summer salads of plain lettuce, beloved by the ancient Egyptians and venerated by them as sacred luck-bringing food of the goddess of increase, Min.

Poppyseeds, now tumbling like black rain from the many papery globes in the garden and field, were assiduously collected for use as a flavouring in cakes, bread and biscuits. Honey, being an excellent natural preservative, was also gathered for use in cooking cakes and biscuits, to be stored in airtight containers in the larder.

In ancient Greece, priestesses called *melissae*, the bees, offered honey and fig cakes to the powerful earth and fertility mother goddesses Rhea and Demeter, and to Iris, goddess of the dawn. In ancient cultures, rich summer honey was always considered an honouring food to serve to guests and dignitaries. In Euripides' *Cretan Women*, the dessert on offer consists of:

> Cheese-cakes, steeped most thoroughly
> In the rich honey of the golden bee.

Throughout Europe from medieval times to at least the late eighteenth century the bee-house had a central, important position in any large kitchen garden, often being very decorative, adorned with turrets and weathervanes. In France beehives were sometimes made of stems of the wild clematis, known as *le berceau de la Vièrge*, 'the bower of the Virgin'. Keeping the bees dry and warm and giving them treats like dishes of sugared water was the duty of the lady of the house. Indeed, in his inappropriately named *Husbandry of Bees*, published in 1617, gardening writer William Lawson proclaims without irony: 'I will not account her any of my good House-wives that wanteth either Bees or skilfulness about them.'

Near the bee-house was often a similarly ornamental dovecote, the residence of the household's white doves which supplemented the household's diet in the winter. The dove is a recurrent symbol in female mythology and religion, being associated with the celestial goddess and fertility symbol the Minoan Great Mother, the western Asian cult goddess Astarte, Aphrodite/Venus, and the Teutonic deity Freya as well as the Virgin Mary.

* * *

For most country women, July meant a hike into the heaths and woodlands gathering ferns to make into lye as a strong whitening agent for the laundry (the soapwort plant was used for delicate stuffs). Dried and burned to ashes, the plant residues were mixed with water and rolled into little balls for use throughout the year. Ferns were also used for dyeing clothes and linens, as were woad, weld, agrimony, safflower, madder and dyer's chamomile, which were gathered this month. Even the poorest housewife was versed in the alchemy of colour-fixing with mordants as well as the subtle room-perfuming arts of potpourri, used by women to fragrance their living space as far back as ancient Egypt.

Take three handsful of orange-flowers, three of clove-gilly flowers, three of damask roses, one of knotted marjoram, one of myrtle, half one of mint, one of lavender, the rind of a lemon, and a quarter of an ounce of cloves. Chop all and put them in layers, with pounded bay-salt between, up to the top of the jar. If all the ingredients cannot be got at once, put them in as you get them; always throwing in salt with every new article.

Domestic Cookery, 1834

Armed with her mortar and pestle, plus spices, herbs, petals, and fixatives such as orris-root powder, storax and benzoin, the mistress of the stillroom would also fill a little silver pomander with 'rose petals, powdered mint and cloves to cheer the soul'. This would be attached to the belt at her waist, from which hung her *chatelaine*, a collective term for her other badges of office: scissors, pincers, bodkin, nutmeg-grater, ear-picker, keys, sheathed knives and purse.

July was the month to gather lavender and the aromatic, insect-repelling herb alecost to put in the linen-press or cupboard, and in both England and France to harvest the tutsan herb (from the Fench teute-saine, 'all-healthy'), whose sweet, dried leaves perfumed many family heirloom Bibles and prayer books. Musty rooms were freshened by burning an incense of magical angelica root (so named because it was believed it could cast out devils) – 'a powerful corrective of putrid air' says PJ Buchoz in the eighteenth-century *The Toilet of Flora*.

In Wales, women made decorative patterns on the floor with red paint and elder leaves. Floors elsewhere were rubbed with pungent rue to prevent witches landing on them, and strewn with sweet dame's violet, meadowsweet and calamus rushes. The fragrant effect was somewhat negated by the habit of hanging strings of onions round rooms to 'absorb pestilential airs'!

Calamus, a fragrant sedge much used on the floor of churches, was carried to the local chapel by young girls dressed in green in a July 'rush-bearing' procession. The rushes were strewn on the floor of the church for aromatic reasons and because it was believed that they warded off pestilence in the congregation.

In the summer, motes of dust were very visible in the sunlit air of the house. Dusting of delicate objects and mirrors was sometimes done with a goose-wing to minimise the risk of breakage, for if a mirror were broken or cracked, seven years of bad luck would be attracted. If such a catastrophe occurred, the sensible householder would avert disaster by running outside and burying the pieces without looking at them. Dust and the male of the species do not mix, according to one Dr Andrew Boorde and his solemnly misogynistic tome of 1547, *The Dietary of Health*:

> Swepynge of houses and chambres ought not to be done as long as any honest man is within the precyncts of the house, for the dust doth putrefye the ayre making it dense.

* * *

Much fortune-telling was done by the July moon as well as the astrology/astronomy of the heavenly constellations. When the new crescent of Artemis/Arianrod (Welsh moon goddess) appeared in the sky, the custom was to bow, turn round three times and curtsy. A popular moon rhyme to be said during a new moon went 'Hoping this night my true love to see, I place my shoes in the form of a T.'

In full-moon young women would brave the 'airy-mice' (bats) and creep outside to put snails in a dish to see if the creature traced the initials of their desired lover. No one, however, would go near a crossroads in a dark, waxing moon phase for fear of meeting Hecate, Queen of the Night, with her huge dogs and burning torches and her messenger, the all-seeing owl.

August

The eighth was August, being richly arrayed
In garment all of gold down to the ground:
Yet rode he not, but led a lovely maid
Forth by the lily hand, the which was crowned
With ears of corn, and full her hand was found
That was the righteous Virgin, which of old
Lived here on earth, and plenty made abound ...

Edmund Spenser

Of choicest flowers, a garland to adorn
Her tresses, and her rural labours crown
As reapers oft are wont their harvest queen.

John Milton describing Eve in Paradise Lost

The last in-gathering of the crop
Is loaded, and they climb the top
And there huzza with all their force,
While Ceres mounts the foremost horse;
'Gee-up!' the rustic goddess cries,
And shouts more long and loud arise;
The swaggering cart, with motion slow,
Reels careless on, and off they go!

Hone's Everyday Book, W Hone, 1802

Ceres, most bountiful lady! Thy rich leas
Of wheat, rye, barley, vetches, oats and pease.
The Tempest, William Shakespeare

Now harvest is ended and supper is past,
Here's our mistress's good health boys,
Come drink a full glass;
For she is a good woman, she provides us
Good cheer,
Here's your mistress's good health, boys,
Come drink off your beer.
Traditional English harvest
toast to the farmer's wife

Salad

When you have lunch at the play-house you will want a nice
salad. Your Lettuces must be perfectly clean and quite dry. You
must have ready on a plate three little heaps of chopped herbs
– Tarragon, Chervil, and some kind of Onion, chopped very
small.
Children and Gardens, Gertrude Jekyll

Bring me an unguent made of scented roots,
Pomander of green herbs and scarlet fruits.
Mary Webb, nineteenth century

Lotion to Allay Heat and Irritation of the Skin

2 oz. lettuce juice, 2 drops of eau de Cologne, 2 oz. distilled
vinegar, 4 oz. elderflower water, well mixed. Dab the skin with
it frequently.
Household Wrinkles, Mrs De Salis, 1890

Come, buy my spice-gingerbread, smoking hot, hot!
Cry of the gingerbread-women

n medieval times the first of August was the official beginning of autumn, when housewives would be looking to preserve and store their succulent summer fruit and vegetables against the hardships of winter. But throughout Europe, August is mainly associated with the rich gold corn harvests, where anciently men did the reaping and women the tying and stooking (plus later the gleaning and threshing). This harvest has long been considered sacred – the ancient Greek initiations into divine wisdom and secret fertility rites known as the Eleusinian Mysteries had as their symbol ears of corn.

In England, 1 August bears the Anglo-Saxon name of Lammas, from hlafmaesse, or loaf mass, when bread made from the new corn was offered in churches for the sacrament. The word 'lady' has the same origins – hlaf-dig, or 'bread dispenser' – from the days when the mistress of the house was the person who gave each individual in the household their daily share of bread.

The harvest was, before the advent of extensive farm mechanisation, steeped in rituals directly descended from the cult of the Sumerian/Greek/Roman grain deities Inanna/Demeter/Ceres. In rural Britain until Victorian times it was believed that the regenerative corn spirit retreated into the last stand of corn as the crop was scythed. A curious plaited and woven figure known as the auld wife, corn dolly or kern baby was made from it. Decked with talismanic red ribbons and held by a girl voted 'Harvest Queen', the corn spirit was carried back to the farm with the last load of corn on a cart decorated with oak and ash boughs and rowan crosses and pulled by flower-garlanded horses with red-ribbon plaited manes. The corn dolly was enthroned in her own special chair for the Harvest Supper. It was considered essential for the well-being of the family and future crops that this magical fetish be kept safe and sound in the kitchen until next year's harvest was safely gathered.

Among the corn-gathering taboos was the firm belief that to wilfully scythe or pick whole poppies was to court bad luck and invoke a storm. If the sky looked threatening, country women would invoke St Helen, whose saint's day was on 18 August. Although officially canonised as the mother of Constantine, first Christian emperor of Rome, Helen – whose origins, according to legend, were in Britain – is also linked with Elen, a Celtic pagan water goddess with power over thunder and lightning.

Like the 'drapery bee' which gathers the vivid poppy petals to line its cell, girls plucked petals here and there to make rich ruby dye for their winter clothes. Scarlet poppies – which, according to Elizabethan gardening by the zodiac, are astrologically flowers of the moon – are also the mythological emblem of Demeter, harvest goddess, and her seed-protective daughter Persephone. Cybele, Phrygian-Greek mother of the gods, is often portrayed wearing a crown of poppies, whose numerous seeds represent her fertility and also, being black, are tokens of Nyx, goddess of night. It has been a popular harvest pastime since antiquity for young women to practise love divination with the crackling leaves of poppies – Margaret searches for one to test the devotion of Faust:

> And that scarlet poppies around like a bower,
> The maiden found her mystic flower.
> *Dr Faustus*, Christopher Marlowe, 1616

If it had been a good summer the Harvest Supper was a gargantuan feast. Prepared by the woman farmer, her daughters, maids and friends for all the workers who had helped garner the crop and get it safely into the barn, it was one of the most popular events of the country year. Homemade cider, mead, gooseberry wine and herb beer washed down great quantities of meat, cheese, pies, syllabubs, plum pudding and sheaf-shaped loaves decorated with 'ear of wheat' plaits and scatterings of seeds.

When not busy with the corn, women spent much of their time in the orchard, gathering apples, pears and plums from the hoary, lichen-clad family trees. The siting of an orchard was therefore of paramount importance. Elizabeth Watts said in her 1885 book *The Orchard and Fruit Garden*: 'The best situation for an orchard or fruit garden is a gentle slope towards the South, South-East, or East – with regard to soil, good corn land is said to do well for fruit.'

Apple trees, under the aegis of the Apple-Mothers, Greek Hera (the mother-goddess with a life-giving apple tree in her garden), and the Roman fruit-tree goddess Pomona, represent eternal life and knowledge. The mandala, pentacle or five-pointed star at the core (from Kore, 'The Maiden', an earlier name for Persephone) of a cut apple was considered a symbol of its mystical qualities, and young women in many cultures and times have tried to read the initials of their future lovers from fallen spirals of apple peel. Roasted apples and sugar was a popular August dish, cooked always with caraway seeds, an ingredient included not only for its freshening effect upon the breath but for its magical qualities in preventing infidelity.

Orchards were frequently surrounded by carefully interwoven spiky wands of bramble, so that succulent blackberries could be picked at the same time as apples, crab-apples and apple-bark (used as a tan/pink dye). Blackberry juice was an old country remedy for summer diarrhoea, and children with whooping cough were made to crawl nine times under archways of bramble in the firm belief this would cure the complaint. To dream of passing through bramble thickets unscratched was very lucky, for it meant the dreamer would triumph over adversaries. In France, autumnal orchards were presided over by beautiful green-clad fertility sprites called *Dames Vertes*, who arrived on the breeze to ripen late fruit.

Mulberry trees, sacred to Minerva in Roman times, dripped their dusky red juice over eager fruit-collectors in many orchards. Women and children gathering windfall apples and pears had to check them carefully for burrowing wasps and, if stung, reach for poppy leaves to rub on for prompt relief. This is also the season for swarms of luck-bringing ladybirds, which should never be brushed from the clothes but always allowed to fly away of their own accord. The more spots on the insect and the deeper red its hue, the more fortune-favoured the person alighted upon.

With the tell-tale signs of winter round the corner – dying hedgerow flowers, birds in moult ready for migration – the race was on to harvest the bounty of over-ripe soft fruits and late herbs, and to hoard and squirrel them away in larder, stillroom, cellar and attic in the form of wines, ciders, preserves, salves, scents and medicine. This was the month of the Festival of the Moon Goddess Hathor/Hecate and her Roman descendant Diana, when women offered the goddess honey and apples. The Christianised version is the Assumption of the Virgin Mary on 15 August. In Germany, the month after this holy feast day is known as 'The Lady's Thirty', the official time for gathering herbs for winter physic and simples. It has always been customary there for more than 70 different herbs to be presented by women at the altar of Our Lady for blessing.

* * *

Among the botanical bounty of August collected in England were aniseed, fenugreek, mustard-seeds for toothache and wormwood-seeds for menstrual pain as advised in the ancient world by female physician Trotula of Salerno. It was most important to keep the seeds dry; indeed:

> Seeds must be gathered in fair weather, at the wane of the Moon, and Kept in some Boxes of Wood, some in bags of Leather, and some in vessels of Earthenware, and well Cleansed and dried in Shadow.
>
> *The English Hus-wife*, Gervase Markham, 1615

Feverfew was picked as an antidote for headaches, vertigo and, according to John Gerard 'for such as be sad, pensive and without speech'. 'Melancholic vapours of the heart' were also treated with motherwort, which blooms in August. Mrs Leyel's 1937 compendium *Green Medicine* gives a recipe which 'braces up the uterine membranes, and relieves nervous irritability':

Conserve of Motherwort

Gather the flowers on a dry day and strip them from the stems – allowing 2 pounds of sugar to 1 pound of flowers. Beat them together in a mortar, stirring the sugar in gradually, then pot and tie down well.

Mallow-root was gathered for teething babies; yarrow was used for healing cuts and as a women's magical protective amulet (it is a herb under the astrological dominion of Venus) – 'Where yarrow grows there is one who knows', ran an old saying. The back-garden harvest included skullcap for infertility and saffron stigmas (sacred to the sun in ancient Egypt and the Crescent Moon goddess in Phoenicia) for golden dyes, divination tea, consumption, asthma and measles cures, and to perk up moulting canaries. It was also considered a most cheering powder, sometimes indeed causing 'immoderate mirth'. A grave gentleman called Tournefort is reported in Margaret Baker's 1928 classic *Discovering the Folklore of Plants* as seeing a lady from Trent 'almost shaken to pieces with laughing immoderately for a space of three hours, which was occasioned by too much Saffron'.

Tough, springy, subtly aromatic Roman chamomile was much used in the garden for edging, paths and rustic seats in herbers. The little white flowers were gathered in August for use as a strewing herb along with aromatic hops 'to clear noxious aires' in the house; for making into sedative, stomach-settling tea; for stuffing into children's 'sleep pillows'; for a blond hair rinse; and for making into unguents and syrups for 'women's complaints'. The plant's botanical name, *Matricaria*, is derived from the Latin *matrix* ('womb/mother') because of its ancient usage for this latter purpose, and since early Christian times the plant has been dedicated to St Anne, mother of the Virgin Mary.

At this time of year, when ordinary plants are on the wane, many waterplants are at their most beautiful. Among the water violets, water-plantain and water flags, women searched for the white flowering water-lily (*Nymphaea*, after Nymphe, the Greek goddess of springs), used as a poultice for vaginal inflammation as well as a pimple and freckle remover. The plant belongs to the same species as the sacred lotus of the Egyptians, which was burned and inhaled as a narcotic. In medieval Europe, the water-lily was an emblem of female 'purity'.

Kitchen hearths and rafters were festooned with strings of soft, leathery drying apple and pear rings, as well as drying herbs and flowers: sage for teeth-whitening; lavender, lemon verbena and scented geranium for strewing in sugar and to put among the linen; pennyroyal to repel fleas; and the silver moons of the dried seed pods of honesty (lunaria) for bewitchment potions, as Lammastide was one of the many special seasons of the year when spirits were thought to walk abroad:

> Enchanting Lunarie here lies,
> In sorceries excelling.
>
> Michael Drayton

Honeycombs in hives were raided on St Bartholomew's Day, 24 August, for beeswax was needed to make polishes and salves for furniture, as well as stoppers and seals for the bottles and jars waiting in the larder and stillroom to capture the taste and smell of summer. Honey was used in many preparations as an emollient and preservative, and its precious sweetness was used in the days before readily available sugar to make many exotic medicinal concoctions taste agreeable! The preservative qualities of honey made it invaluable in ham-curing, to candy edible roots and to make bottled preserves last through the barren winter.

It was thought that fruit yields were at their best during the full moon, so preserves were usually made at this time. When sticky jams, pastes and pickles of damson, quince, medlar, rowanberry, nasturtium seed and what have you were bubbling over the fire in the gleaming copper preserving pan they were, of course, always stirred sunwise in the old Druid way, as were the botanic beers and wines made this month.

One of the most popular pan-European sweetmeats for the winter was fruit 'cheese', made of honey and dried fruit pulp, cut into squares or diamonds and decorated with crystallised flowers.

The shelves groaning with jewel-like jars of jellies, preserves and lucent stillroom syrups; vinegars infusing rosemary and blackberries on sunny windowsills; the sweet, evocative scent of stored apples; the great twisted ropes of onions and garlic; the heavy hessian sacks of loamy potatoes; the string bags of giant striped marrows – all this harvest, both cultivated and wild, was in the careful custody of its 'curator', the mistress of the house. In Roman times the Penates, the guardian deities of the store-cupboard, also kept a watchful eye on the family produce.

In August, women and children gathered dry, small pieces of fallen ash wood or young willow from which to whittle clothes-pegs. Large household items were washed now, when good weather could be more or less guaranteed. In some places it was thought most unlucky for water to be spilt between the well/spring and the wash-tub, so excellent deportment was required from the water-carrier.

Heather, golden-rod and walnuts were gathered now for dyeing, and dried teasels were collected, their spines used for raising the nap on spun wool. Flax and wool were sorted for spinning and weaving in the winter months. Lammastide was the time to gather rushes for winter lighting – the green then had to be peeled off the pith, which then soaked up tallow, beeswax, mutton-fat or fish-oil.

* * *

After doing lots of hot, sweaty work in the fields and garden, feet washing was often a priority when people came home in the evening. A corn-softening salve of bread, ivy leaves and vinegar was sometimes on standby, as were bowls of soothing herbal water – but woe betide anyone who left their shoes crossed on the floor, or worse still, put them on the table, for this could portend a death in the family, or an unwanted pregnancy.

Foot Bath
Take 4 handfuls of Pennyroyal, Sage, Rosemary, 3 handfuls of Angelica and 4 ounces of Juniper berries; boil these ingredients in a sufficient quantity of water and strain off the liquid for use.

The Toilet of Flora, PJ Buchoz, 1784

Women usually brought a jar or bottle from their own produce harvest when they visited a friend, and went home with something from the pantry or stillroom of the hostess. An old country ruse of ensuring the friendship of a new acquaintance was to surreptitiously slip a slice of lemon under her chair. If a fly fell into someone's tea on such an occasion, this was an omen of good fortune. The tea, of course, was never stirred anti-clockwise, as this was the devil's way. If when the hostess went into her cellar or pantry she found a frog, it was ill-starred to harm it – this dates back to Roman times when this amphibian was a foetus-symbol representing fertility and plenty, under the aegis of Venus.

Because of all the other activities going on this month, dusting and polishing was not high on the household agenda. A useful housework elf was a great bonus – and most western European countries had their own legendary ethereal aides willing to scrub and flick a duster in exchange for a saucer of milk or a piece of cake. Spain and Portugal, for example, boasted the slavish *Duende*; southern Germany and Austria the *Wichtln*; Wales the *Bwciod*, and England the Brownie and Pixie.

With or without magical assistance the family cutlery had to be cleaned in case a visitor needed a spoon to taste one of the new preserves. In Tudor times wealthy women possessed a set of silver 'Maidenhead Spoons' which had tiny figures of the Virgin Mary set on top of the handle. Other special family metalware that had to be kept gleaming included the symbolic horse-brasses (often shaped like a wheatsheaf inside a circle), which were hung as good-luck charms over the hearth when the horses had safely brought home the corn harvest.

A very important August task because of the bulk manufacture of medicines, preserved foodstuffs and harvest fare was the purchasing of foreign gums and resins for the stillroom as well as spices to re-stock the many tiny drawers of the family's precious spicery cabinet. Spices were used very liberally in fragrant distillations for physic, as well as for sweet and savoury culinary dishes in the houses of the well-to-do. Queen Elizabeth I was devoted to her daily 'comfits', little lozenges made of ginger, aniseed, caraway and fennel seeds. Ginger was especially important this month because it was used very liberally in making gingerbread which was sold at revels, fêtes and the hiring fairs where house- and farm-workers offered their services to prospective new employers for the next season.

> And had I one penny in the world thou
> Should'st have it to buy gingerbread.
> *Love's Labour's Lost*, William Shakespeare

Gingerbread biscuits, known as 'fairings', were made sometimes in the shapes of buttons and patterns – rich households had their own gingerbread moulds embossed with their coat of arms. Gingerbread animals and people (there were whole gingerbread families: husbands, wives and children) were sold on many stalls and were a popular lover's gift. In medieval times, gilded 'red' and 'white' gingerbread was the favourite universal sweetmeat. Each fairing was carefully decorated with a box leaf, signifying longevity, and stuck through with a clove. Sometimes the gingerbread was stamped with the image of a popular saint.

Coarse Gingerbread

Take a quart of Honie clarified, and seeth it till it be browne, and if it be thicke, put to it a dish of water; then take fine crummes of white bread grated and put to it, and stirre it well, and when it is almost cold, put to it the powder of Ginger, Cloves, and Cinnamon and a little Licoras and Aniseeds: then knead it and put it in moulds and print it: some use to put to it also a little Pepper, but that is according to taste and pleasure.

Country Contentments, Gervase Markham, 1623

Country women sometimes bought their spices from travelling pedlar-women, who often told fortunes as well. One of the main purchases from pedlars were pins, much used in divination and protective magic as well as for practical purposes. Would-be visitors with evil intent were kept from entering by sticking pins in the door-post, and she who wished ill to her husband and/or lover was careful to wear nine pins concealed about her person.

Another popular purchase was little coloured silken handkerchiefs, which young women then embroidered with a button or tassel at each corner and one in the centre. Wrought with the beloved's name, these 'true-love's knots' were much worn at the autumn hiring fairs. According to a nineteenth-century almanac, 'the finest of these favours were edged with narrow gold lace, or twist; and then, being folded up in four cross folds, so that the middle might be seen, they were worn by the accepted lovers in their hats, or at the breasts'.

At the end of the month, in the astrological time of the goddess Virgo, with her emblem of the five ears of wheat in a sheaf, silk handkerchiefs were also used as equipment for love prognostication. Looking at a still lake or pond with a full moon behind her, a woman would hold the silk square in front of her. The number of moon reflections cast in the water represented the number of months she had to wait before she met the person of her dreams. Clairvoyants also used the light of the full moon on still water for scrying their visions.

September

They made a good deal of camomile tea ... A large jug of this was always prepared and stood ready for heating up after confinements.

Lark Rise to Candleford, Flora Thompson, 1945

A lovely boy stol'n from an Indian King,
She never had so sweet a changeling.
  A Midsummer Night's Dream, William Shakespeare

Thyme ... being a notable herb of Venus, provokes the terms, gives a safe and speedy delivery to women in travail, and brings away the afterbirth.

Herbal, Nicholas Culpepper, 1653

*A Medicine to break and heale sore breasts of Women, used by
Mid-Wives, and other skillfull Women in London:*
Boyle Oatmeale, of the smallest you can get, and red Sage together, in running or Conduict water, till it be thick enough to make a Plaister, and then put into it a fit proportion of Honey, and let it boyle a little together, take it off the fire, and while it is yet boyling hot, put thereto so much of the best Venice Terpentine as will make it thick enough to spread, then spreading it on some soft leather, or a good thick linen

cloath, apply it to the brest, and it will break the soare, and after that being continued, will also heal it up.

> *A Book of Fruits and Flowers*, Anon, 1653

You willed me to go to Mistress M's Churching, and when I came thither I found great cheer and no small company of wives.

> *The Batchelor's Banquet*, Thomas Dekker, 1603

She must be discreet, wary-eyed, tactful and sympathetic to the woman.

> Soranus of Ephesus defining the role of
> the midwife, 200 AD

> Philomel, with lullaby
> Sing in our sweet lullaby;
> Lulla, lulla, lullaby; lulla, lulla, lullaby ...
> *A Midsummer Night's Dream*, William Shakespeare

A family of ten children will be always called a fine family, when there are heads and arms and legs enough for the number.

> *Northanger Abbey*, Jane Austen
> (published posthumously, 1818)

'He'll mend of his youngness with time,' said Martha.

> *Five Children and It*, E Nesbit, 1902

> The Queen of Hearts,
> She made some tarts,
> All on a summer's day.
> Mother Goose nursery rhyme

eptember, nine months after the revels of Christmas, is a month when many women through the ages have been focused on garnering a different aspect of nature's ripe fruit harvest – the burgeoning new life within their own bodies. The physiological demands of childbirth have always been the same for every woman, whatever her culture. Slaves in ancient Egypt squatted on two stones to give birth, while queens such as Cleopatra squatted too, albeit on a gilded birthing stool painted with the image of the pregnancy protectors: the cat-headed goddess Bast or the cow-mother of the sun, Hathor. September, Hathor's month, was the beginning of the New Year in ancient Egypt, when priestesses dressed as the fecund goddess paraded the streets playing the tabor.

Every culture and every age has seen pregnancy and childbirth as mysterious and magical, enshrining them with complex mythology and folklore. Until just before the middle of this century it was usual for women of every station to give birth 'secretly' at home, attended by an all-female coterie of mother, sisters and close friends plus the local midwife.

This month of atmospheric, misty mornings witnesses the Autumnal Equinox, when day and night are equal in the sky. The Eleusinian Mysteries took place now – Athenian women went in procession to the temple bearing Ceres' comb and mirror, plus honey, figs, and pomegranates signifying fertility and immortality.

The September night sky has always been of particular significance to women. It was considered sacrilegious to try and count the stars in the night sky belonging to Astraea the 'Starry One' (later known as Virgo). Artemis, as a lunar deity, was the patron of nurture and birth, while Hygeia and Panacea, daughters of the doctor-god Asclepius, looked after the heavenly apothecary which soothed those who sought its cures *in extremis*.

Women in antiquity took a variety of lotions and potions to avoid miscarriage, including tincture of ox-eye daisy, dedicated to Eileithuia, Greek goddess of womanly functions. The female healer Aspasia, writing in the first century AD, advised avoiding chariot rides when pregnant, and recommended vaginal suppositories of mallow and flax.

In medieval Europe pregnant women ate the perfumed flesh of the quince (the golden 'apple' of legend, sacred to Venus and Aphrodite) in the belief that it made their unborn child more intelligent. Morning sickness was coped with through the centuries with wafer-thin ginger biscuits or infusions of lavender, a herb sacred in plant mythology to both Hecate and the Virgin Mary. There were many ruses and remedies throughout the ages to make the heavy burden of pregnancy more comfortable – one of the most eccentric in the seventeenth century was for the woman to wear a hoop round her neck and under her 'bulge' while at home near the birth time to support the weight of her baby.

Many exotic concoctions were used to ease the pangs of child-birth – from columbine seeds in wine to syrups made from night scented stock, marshmallow, pasque flower, marigold or jasmine. 'Pain cakes' were sometimes made out of hempseed, egg, milk, dandelion and rhubarb root, mixed with gin. Vervain – dedicated by the Romans to Isis, the goddess of birth, and sacred herb of the Druid wizards – was recommended by Nicholas Culpeper as a womb herb for its ability in 'opening obstructions'.

Confined to her lying-in chamber, the expectant mother protected herself from any impending misfortune by wearing a red silk belt embroidered with mystical figures, or repeatedly reciting the Magnificat. One of the commonest protective amulets in use (still in use, in fact, until the early part of this century) was a dark-coloured, heart-shaped rock called an eagle-stone (from the belief that eagles used them in the construction of their nests). Women strapped the stones to their inner thighs in a garter to protect against a 'painefull travayle' when labour began. They also wore anti-witchcraft rowanberry necklaces, and/or held a 'magnetic' gemstone charm such as jasper or red carnelian, as recommended by Benedictine abbess Hildegard of Bingen, who was born on 17 September. A pair of open scissors placed under the bed symbolised cutting through the pain.

When labour proper began (alchemilla or lady's mantle herb was used to stimulate contractions), midwives went around the house making sure all the doors were unlocked and all knotted items and articles of clothing were undone, as a metaphor for an easy birth. In Victorian times a white cloth was tied around the door-knocker to muffle the sound and alert neighbours to the woman's 'interesting state'.

Lavender flowers were burned in the fire or on a brazier to aromatise and sanitise the birthing room, which in England was invariably on the ground floor. This was so that the baby could symbolically 'go up in the world' by being carried upstairs by a family member or midwife. If there was no upstairs, the midwife often stepped with the baby onto a box to achieve an elevation, however slight. In Greece, up until the middle of this century, it was common for grandmothers to place teaspoons of orange, vanilla and cherry syrup next to the newborn to 'sweeten' the Fates and make them smile kindly on the child.

In the West Country of England there was an old superstition that a woman with sore breasts could effect a cure by making a heart-shaped amulet from the lead of a church window. Easier, less vandalistic remedies were red clover or chickweed ointment, daisy or blessed thistle juice. A poultice of violet leaves and breadcrumbs was prescribed by midwives and wise-women for cracked nipples and engorgement.

Take Fennel seeds bruised, and boil them well in Barley Water, whereof let wet Nurses and Suckling Women drink very often, in Winter warm, in Summer cold, and let them beware of drinking much strong Beer, Ale or Wine, for they are hot, and great drier's up of Milk, and so are all Spices and to much Salt, or salt meat.

The Queen's Closet Opened, WM, 1655

In England the newborn was sometimes sprinkled with water from a holly twig, a remnant of a Druidic ritual, and garlanded with a necklace made of peony root or seeds gathered in the wane of the moon, to protect it against being stolen by fairies and replaced with a changeling. A spoonful of sap from the highly regarded magical ash tree was frequently a child's first worldly nourishment in the Highlands and Islands of Scotland. As honey was considered the life-giving, prophetic food of the gods in ancient Greece, newborns were given it before they took their mother's milk. Honey straight from the hive mixed with salt was used as an abrasive rub for newborns in some parts of Britain. It was considered doubly lucky if a bee flew round the child's cradle, which should for good luck contain primroses (fresh or dried), heather and a crust of bread.

Inauspicious acts included a baby seeing itself in the mirror in the first year of its life, and being weighed during the same period. Pieces of dried umbilical cord were sometimes kept by mothers and worn as a ring or in a locket with a curl of the baby's first hair, as a charm to give the infant the same protection he/she had when still *in utero*. In the first year mothers usually bit their babies' nails short rather than cutting them, part of a complex mystique about nail-cutting. When the scissors were finally used, there was a fortune-telling rhyme to go with the cutting ritual:

> Cut them on Monday, cut them for wealth;
> Cut them on Tuesday, cut them for health;
> Cut them on Wednesday, cut them for news;
> Cut them on Thursday, a new pair of shoes;
> Cut them on Friday, cut them for woe;
> Cut them on Saturday, a journey to go;
> Cut them on Sunday, cut them for evil,
> And be all week as cross as the Devil.

Anon

Until she had been to church to give thanks for the safe birth of her child, a woman was not considered 'pure' enough to fulfil any social engagement. At their 'churching', some women walked sunwise round the church to additionally ensure that no future misfortune befell them and their offspring. Cradles were made of sacred oak, or in France, hawthorn, whose wood was once used for the torches that illuminated the altar in the temple of Hymen. Usually a citrus pomander rubbed with spices and spiked with cloves hung from the cradle to ward off infection.

It was usual in many parts of Europe for the baby's christening cake to be a specially saved layer of its mother's wedding cake. In some parts of Germany and Austria it was believed that if a girl was baptised straight after a boy without fresh holy water being used, the infant was in danger of being bearded when she grew up! Traditional christening gifts included silver spoons with apostle figures on the handles, and necklaces and amulets made from sprigs of protective red coral or green malachite – symbols of eternal spring. After the christening party, it was customary for a woman to give an informal tea for her female friends and neighbours. On departing, guests of child-bearing age had to jump over a bucket in which sat a lighted candle. If the candle went out, or the woman stumbled, this was taken to mean that she would be pregnant soon.

Little children were not told the facts about procreation – it was common for siblings in Scandinavia and Holland to be told a stork had brought the baby. In Britain children were told that the new baby had been found in a parsley bed if a boy, or under a gooseberry bush if a girl. In children's culture a shooting star in the sky was the soul of a new baby coming to earth from the heavens. Small bowls of sugar were left on the windowsill in Middle Europe if the mother was desperate for a girl baby, poppy seeds if she wanted a boy.

Predicting the sex of the impending new arrival used to be a popular parlour pastime. One of the most common rituals was holding a piece of cotton over the abdomen of the mother-to-be. If the cotton moved, the baby was declared to be a boy; if it stayed still, a girl. It was believed in many places that a child born between midnight on a Friday and dawn on Saturday would be clairvoyant and also have the ability to see ghosts and fairies.

> Three little ghostesses,
> Sitting on postesses,
> Eating buttered toastesses.
>
> Traditional children's nursery rhyme

The significance of birth circumstances in prognostication was immense – 'footling' or breech birth babies were said to have the power to heal, and babies born with a caul (a soft veil of membrane) over their heads could never drown or be destroyed by fire. An old wives' tale says that the seventh child of a seventh child has not only good fortune but supernatural powers.

Few mothers would dare to wean a child during a waning harvest moon, in case the child's health also dwindled and faded. Milk is notoriously difficult to suppress in September, for the Milky Way – formed, according to legend, from drops of Hera's milk as she suckled Heracles – is now particularly vivid and clear in the night sky. Weaning tea, drunk by many generations of mothers in areas of Britain, France and Germany usually contained sage leaves to dry up the milk.

Any infant teething problems were soothed with the help of homemade teething rings made of marshmallow root, rock-hard homemade bread rusks and rowan-wood pegs as well as dosages of poppy syrup or tea.

The child's first birthday was of enormous significance in times with much neo-natal and infant mortality. The concept of a birthday cake decorated with candles has its origin in celebrations for the birth of the ancient Greek moon goddess Artemis, at which worshippers carried moon-shaped cakes and blew out altar candles with one breath to emphasise the power of moonlight.

* * *

Much baking was done in September. In well-to-do homes, baked goods were coloured with the dried yellow stigmas of the crocus, and in peasant households by crumbled marigold petals. If there was ever any leftover dough it was considered bad luck to waste it. Tiny cakes or tarts for the children were usually made out of any excess, with a pastry star or moon a popular decoration in many countries. 'Revel buns' made to be sold at this month's village 'revels' or hiring fairs were coloured with saffron and cooked in sycamore leaves. At glove fairs in medieval times young women from wealthy families gave friends and lovers gloves as emblems of generosity.

The sweet chestnut harvest is a French September feature, with the nuts dried and milled to make flour or candied in *marrons glacés*. Nutting Day officially began in the woods and forests of England on 3 September, with women and children collecting hazelnuts for flour (the hazel is a Druid fertility tree) and walnuts for pickling to eat with winter cheese. However, everyone avoided harvesting autumn nuts on 21 September, for this was known as 'The Devil's Nutting Day'. When out in the woods, girls would tie red ribbons on rowan trees as an anti-witchcraft measure before gathering the brilliant red berries for jam and wine, and rowan twigs to make into crosses to hang above the winter hearth.

Another food-gathering feature of the dank yet often sunny September morning was the harvesting of edible fungi such as field mushrooms, chanterelles, blewets and morels. Puffball mushrooms were picked to burn as bee-pacifiers when the hive was raided of its late honey, and the poisonous red-and-white spotted 'fairy toadstools' of fairy tales – the fly agarics – were sometimes collected to attract and then decimate lingering fly populations in kitchen, barn and dairy.

> My Phyllis me with pelted puff-ball plies;
> Then tripping to the wood the wanton flies.
>
> John Dryden

A great feast-day was held on 29 September – that of Michaelmas, the mass of St Michael and All The Angels. This was the day when all tenants had to pay their quarterly rent. This didn't stop them making merry with a great feast of roast goose made fat by feeding on stubble gleanings. In medieval times the bird was decorated with autumn fruits and flowers and stuffed with prunes and sausagemeat. Later apple and walnut stuffing and gooseberry or sorrel sauce became desirable accoutrements.

> Old Mother Goose,
> When she wanted to wander,
> Would ride through the air
> On a very fine gander ...
>
> Children's nursery rhyme

Nothing was wasted from the Michaelmas bird: the leftover goose fat was either used for cooking or was purified and perfumed and used in face-creams. Bones were carved into bodkins and lace-making bobbins. Ingenious women used other animal bones, particularly marrow bones from stews, for constructing crochet hooks.

After Michaelmas country people were extremely reluctant to eat blackberries, due to the old belief that on Michaelmas Night the devil spits on all the berries.

A popular autumn jam in some English country villages was made of finely shredded carrots with honey and hyssop – it was called 'angel's hair'. The fragrant quince, emblem of fertility and love, was picked now, kept in a warm room to ripen, then made into orange-pink quince paste to give to guests at Christmas. Pears were baked with sugar and cloves or mashed to make sparkling perry wine. The vivid red urns and globes of rose-hips were made into tart-fillings, winter tonics, wine, anti-varicose vein tea, soup, and, with lemons, luscious rose-topaz marmalade.

A good many of the recently gathered apples stored in the attic would now be used in making cider – but it had to be made while the moon was waning or the resulting brew might well be sour. Aromatic, sedative hops were harvested this month and used either for festive garlands for the rafters or in recipes for beer, calming bedtime teas or soothing sleep and/or toothache-pillows. The soft mucilage in quince seeds was painstakingly collected and used in the stillroom for medicines, face-creams and hair-fixatives. Since Roman times women have picked sprays of lush, black-red elderberries not only for jam, headache tinctures, ink and wine, but also to use as an instant hair dye. Lily-of-the-valley leaves picked now yielded a rich golden fabric dye, sorrel tops more subtle pinks and olives.

Mothers, wisewomen and ladies of the manor with responsibility for the health of many people would now make sure they had adequate supplies of folk/herbal medicine to see them and their customers/charges through the bitter winter. Their kitchen cupboard pharmacy would probably include onions (an ancient Egyptian symbol of eternity) for boils and ear-aches, potatoes for rheumatism and sprains, and cabbage leaves to tie around sore throats.

More esoteric concoctions might include spinning-wheel yarn garters for cramp and gout – spinning wheels have been considered magical since ancient times because of their association with Arachne the spider and Athene, spinner of fates. Medicine chests contained such delights as pink elecampane cakes for wheezy children; honeysuckle and marigold oil for chilblains; resin and oil of pine (sacred to the mother of the gods, Cybele), for making into liniments; meadowsweet for fevers; conserve of catmint for nightmares; and elder rob, a sweet cough mixture made from the berries of the magical elder-mother tree. The greater plantain – known as 'Mother of Worts' by the Anglo-Saxons, for whom it was one of nine sacred herbs – was used to staunch wounds. Women who lived on the coastline used bladderwrack, a seaweed, in a powerful and pungent anti-rheumatism tea. Romany women collected vials of poppy juice for use as an anaesthetic and an ingredient in love philtres. Some remedies had purely emotional applications:

Water of Time for the Passions of the Heart
Take a quart of white Wine, and a pint of Sack, steep in it as
much broad Thime as it will wet, put to it Galingale and
Calamus Aromaticus, of each one ounce, Cloves, Mace,
Ginger, and grains of Paradise two drams, steep there all
night, the next morning distill it in an ordinary still, drink it
warm with Sugar.

The Queen's Closet Opened, WM, 1655

* * *

Many housewives now started making plaited garlic ropes,
establishing an indoor windowsill winter herb-garden of
marjoram, chives and parsley, and tying trimmings of lavender,
rosemary, thyme and sage in small bundles to enliven and
aromatise winter fires. A bunch of hazel twigs, tied with a
woman's hair, was a fireplace-mantel talisman meant to keep the
house safe from destruction by fire and lightning. Even rose bush-
prunings weren't thrown away – some people dried them for a
year and then made buttons for the family's clothes out of them.

This autumnal month was a time for airing and cleaning
bedding and warm clothing before the chill of winter arrived.
Hanging the washing out among the first colour-changing
leaves, housewives would look out for the first falling autumn
oak leaf. If they could manage to catch it before it touched the
ground, this was an excellent portent that they would escape a
serious cold in the winter. If the bedding dried quickly on the
line in between showers, this was a certain omen of their true
loves remaining constant. When heavy winter clothes came out
of store in the autumn, they were never put on until the Sunday
of that week, in the belief that this would make them last twice
as long. If any article of clothing was put on inside out by
mistake, the wearer had to walk in a sunwise circle three times
before putting it on again correctly.

October

Soul! Soul! for a soul-cake;
Pray, good mistress, for a soul-cake;
One for Peter, two for Paul,
Three for them that made us all.
Soul! Soul! for an apple or two;
If you've got no apples, give a pear or two.
If you haven't got a pear then God bless you.

Rhyme-chant for All Soul's Night

Heigho for Hallowe'en,
When all the witches are to be seen,
Some in black and some in green,
Heigho for Hallowe'en!

Traditional song

From ghoulies and ghosties and long-legged beasties,
And things that go bump in the night,
Good Lord, deliver us!

Old Cornish prayer

A Thorn or a Burr
She takes for a Spur:

With a lash of a Bramble she rides now,
Through Brakes and through Briars,
O'er Ditches and Mires,
She follows the Spirit that guides now.

The Hag, Robert Herrick

Sprigs of lad's love lay among the cloths in the oak presses, and the children at school wore bunches of it to keep them healthy now the damp mists were about.'

The Country Child, Alison Uttley, 1931

Leaves, To Preserve

Stand autumn leaves in a jar with half an inch or so of water and glycerine in equal parts, until the stems have absorbed all the moisture. Then arrange the leaves in a dry vase and they will keep their colour.

Enquire Within, Elizabeth Craig, 1948

There's pippins and cheese to come.

The Merry Wives of Windsor, William Shakespeare

O the bonny woolly sheep,
Feedin' on the mountain steep,
Bleat ye! Bleat ye! as ye go!
Thro' the winter frost and sno',
Hart, nor hind, nor fallow deer,
No by half, so useful are ...

Old spinning song quoted in
The Countryman's England, Dorothy Hartley, 1935

Sloe gin, blended with Pennyroyal and Valerian, has for years been used by country wives in connubial emergencies.

Food in England, Dorothy Hartley, 1954

Fall, leaves, fall; die, flowers, away;
Lengthen night and shorten day:
Every leaf speaks bliss to me
Fluttering from the autumn tree.

Emily Brontë

n Anglo-Saxon times October was called Wintirfyllith, the month of the winter moon, when winter wheat was sown. Festivity and foreboding were often mixed in October, for in the pagan Celtic calendar the end of the month was known as Samhain, 'Summer's End', when merry fire festivals were held to usher in the Celtic New Year and embryonic fertility before the imminent icy weather and times of hardship. Samhain, later Christianised as All Hallow's Eve or Hallowe'en, was also a celebration of the supernatural, a fairy night of magical happenings at the lowest point of the sun's cycle, when it was said the dead walked between the worlds. It was in the medieval period that witches – cultural descendants of the followers of Hecate the magician-moon goddess and Cailleach Bheur the blue-skinned female winter deity of the early Britons – began to be associated with 31 October.

With thick mists swirling round the dankly glowing stands of ancient evergreen yew, country people kept well away from these churchyard trees, symbols of re-birth through death. Once sacred to Hecate and Athene, their branches were said to be favoured ingredients in arcane potions. Indeed, Shakespeare describes the cauldron of the witches in Macbeth as containing 'slips of yew, Silver'd in the Moon's eclipse'.

Among the herbs legendarily used by witches for their Hallowe'en flying ointment were aconite, artemisia, belladonna, calamus, mandrake, saffron, hemlock, water-lily, poppy, valerian and deadly nightshade. The ritual application of a salve made of these hallucinogenic titans of psychopharmacology may well have caused a sensation of soaring into the skies on a broomstick or in a boat made of eggshells! Any self-respecting witch apparently made her Hallowe'en Sabbat broom from 'Hecate's plants' – ash, the anti-drowning wood for the stick, crowned with birch twigs bound by osiers.

Women had the jobs of both protecting the home from the unwelcome Hallowe'en attentions of occult beings with malevolent intent and at the same time signalling respect to any departed ancestors or relatives who might be floating about on this Night of Chaos. Bowls of food and drink were left on the doorstep to placate ghostly relatives who might return home on this evening, in the hope that refreshed, they might go back to the churchyard and not haunt their families. More sinister supernaturals they thwarted with seven grains of salt in a pot of water hung over the fire, leaning the poker upright against the bars of the grate to form the sign of the cross. The fire itself was new and blessed, having been ceremonially lit by a flame carefully carried from the Samhain bonfire. Chimneys were often swept with a holly-bush in honour of the new blaze; this was done by dropping a bush down the chimney on a rope.

Lightning, a terror to those living in wooden or thatched houses, was kept at bay by zig-zag lines painted or carved on the fireplace. Wishes were sometimes written on bay-leaves and cast into the flames, a folk-memory perhaps of the fire-offerings of the sacred hearth of the Greek/Roman goddess Hestia/Vesta. It was considered most disrespectful to point directly at the fire, and coals were observed most carefully for their shape. An oval 'cradle' coal signified a new baby for the finder.

In England, little lanterns made of turnips were carved into grotesque faces, lit and put on windowsills to scare any ghoulies or ghosts. In other parts of northern Europe such as Germany and Scandinavia, women fixed juniper branches and dried marjoram to the front door to protect the house from hostile spirits.

In medieval England 'Soulers' wearing frightening masks went from door to door singing and begging for oatmeal and ginger 'soul cakes' and apples. This may be the origin of our present-day trick-or-treating, but in the past this ritual did not actually happen on Hallowe'en but on All Souls Eve, the night of 1 November.

* * *

Other 'religious' cakes made this month in England included St Faith's cakes, which were grilled over the fire (as, allegedly, was the martyr). These pancake-like delicacies had to be made by three single young women, who would each turn the cake three times as it cooked. Each third of the St Faith's cake was then cut into nine and passed through a silver ring before being eaten. This ritual was observed so that the young women might have a divinatory dream of their future true loves that night.

The Feast of St Ursula, on 21 October, originates in a folk-tale about a British princess who fled Britain for Germany with no fewer than 11,000 handmaidens in order to escape marriage, only for the whole lot of them to be martyred at Cologne. Ursula may be a Christianisation of the Slavic moon goddess Orsel, and indeed sugary Ursuline cakes are traditionally sickle-moon-shaped, like croissants (crescents).

Hallowmass or Hallowe'en was, understandably, a favoured night for divinations of all sorts. Fortune-telling crowdie, a pudding made of apples and cream, contained two rings, two coins and two marbles, prophesying who among the partakers would be wed, wealthy, single or childless. Crowdie spooned out on its own meant an uncertain future. Spirals of apple-parings were also thrown over the left shoulder to see if they fell into the shape of any particular initial; and apples, each named for a loved one and floated in a tub of water, were bobbed for. Seizing the apple at first bite was a very good omen indeed. Apples have much portent on this night, as the fruit was given to all the Norse gods as symbols of immortality by Freya, keeper of love and magic.

Divination games utilising nuts were so popular that Hallowe'en was also known as Nutcrack Night. Would-be lovers put two hazelnuts or walnuts into the red-hot embers of the fire and waited until the shells exploded. Nuts crackling noisily was an excellent sign of vigorous affection, but silent burning boded ill for permanent attraction. This was the nutcrack rhyme recited when the nuts were put in the fire:

If he (or she) loves me, pop and fly;
If he (or she) hates me, lie and die.

Hazelnuts were also ground to make flour for hazel-bread –
thought to be a magical food because of the tree's past association with Druidic religious rituals, and since ancient Greek
times hazel has been linked to fertility and lush growth. Walnuts
similarly had varied uses and properties. Walnut bread was eaten
to cure 'alle sorts of madnesse' and French women for centuries
made a decoction of walnuts to make their eyelashes thick and
glossy.

With plenty of good flour around after the corn harvest,
bread-making was now high on the agenda. From the most
ancient times this has been an activity with pagan sacred
resonances. Until quite recently in rural Europe, it was
unthinkable not to stir the flour mixture sunwise and ornament
the top of the unbaked loaf with a cross, magical knots, runic
signs, a heart shape, or a plaited spiral.

For Celtic peoples as for many others loaves were symbolic
fertility/good-fortune objects as well as food, and in many
cultures a hard piece of bread has been tied to a baby's clothes
not only as a teething aid but also as an amulet against the evil
eye. Powdered breadcrumbs were often used as magical
medicine; country people in France used it against pneumonia.
Stale caraway-seed bread was a popular European country lure
for straying hens.

There were many strict 'rules' associated with bread-making,
including no singing while baking and no other bread being cut
with a knife while the new bread is in the oven. A hole or
'coffin' inside the loaf foretold a death in the family, a split loaf
a quarrel, and woe betide any woman who put a loaf irreverently
upside down on the table!

* * *

Many sloes, cold toes.

Country proverb

October – which although it presages winter also presages new beginnings in the thousands of seeds dispersed in the air – is the last opportunity for in-gathering of autumn fruits from among the skeletal trees. Against the palette of russet tints a sprinkling of hardy apples still hangs; the hedgerows are studded with scarlet hips and haws, violet-black sloes, buckthorn and elderberries.

> Here the industrious housewives wend their way
> Pulling the brittle branches careful down
> And hawking loads of berrys to the town
> With unpretending skill yet half divine
> To press and make their elderberry wine ..
>
> *The Shepherd's Calendar*, John Clare, 1827

The kitchen and store-room were now stacked floor to ceiling with provisions and must have been a magnificent sight – eggs oiled and waxed and stored in sawdust; nuts buried in salt or sand; garlands of hops and cored apples festooned across the ceiling to dry. Hedgerow berries were made into preserves (sloes were also sucked to oust winter mouth ulcers), and for the children there was the treat of 'small windfall apples dipped in a toffee of honey and beeswax'. (*Food in England*, Dorothy Hartley, 1954).

* * *

Romany women would now dig up dandelion roots to grind for a 'coffee' beverage and boil late parsley with sugar to make a honeyish spread. Everywhere housewives used real honey too make mead, but it was polite as well as good bee-management to leave something sweet – such as sugar or cake – for the bees to feed on when honeycombs were removed.

Mead Wine

Take 1 gallon of water to 4 to 5 1b honey, 2 oz of hops to every 10 gallons the above, the rinds of 3 to 4 lemons, a few coriander seeds. Put the water on to heat and when it is hot add the honey and bring to the boil, removing the scum as it rises. Boil for 1 and a half hrs. Add the lemon rinds and coriander seeds, sewn into a bag. Remove from the heat. When cold, put it into a cask, stop it tight and let it store for 9 to 12 months. Then draw off the wine and bottle.

The Female Economist, Mrs Smith, 1810

Autumn cheeses were sometimes coloured with dried marigold petals, and the softer curd ones stored in tightly wrapped rushes.

A Curd Star

Set a quart of new milk upon the fire with two or three blades of Mace; and when ready to boil, put it to the yolks and whites of nine eggs well beaten, and as much salt as will lie upon a small knife's point. Let it boil till the whey is clear; then drain it in a thin cloth, or hair sieve; season it with sugar, and a little cinnamon, rose water, orange-flower water, or white wine, to your taste; and put into star-form, or any other. Let it stand some hours before you turn it into a dish; then put round it thick cream or custard.

A New System of Domestic Cookery, Maria Rundell, 1807

* * *

For the ancient Egyptians, the multilayered onion was a symbol of eternity. Many other cultures have since then used it extensively in medicine and housewifery. French countrywomen used onions to clean their brass dishes, while in England healers known as 'cunning-women' advised their clients to wear grated onion in their socks for chilblains, to rub cut onions on their heads for headaches and hair-loss, and make a cure-all remedy from the strained juice of grated onions and sugar.

A most certin and proved medicine against all manner of pestilence and plague, be it never so vehement
Take an onion, and cut it overthwart, then make a little hole

in either piece, the which you shall fill with fine treacle and set the pieces together as they were before: after this wrap them in a fine wet linnen cloth putting it to roast, and covered in the embers or ashes, and when it is roasted enough press out all the juice of it, and give the patient a spoonful, and immediately he shall feel himself better, and shall without fail be healed.

Recipes and Remedies 1669–1712, Jane Mosley

Hot parsnip pulp poultices were recommended for boils, and a pungent 'change of life' tonic of hops, skullcap, motherwort, gentian and chamomile or, in France, cypress leaves, was brewed up. Orange-peel nostril suppositories were rolled to protect against catching cold, white pepper prescribed to stop bleeding, and rowan-berry syrup doled out to prevent scurvy. The rowan tree and its fruit were thought to have many useful properties in addition to scurvy prevention. Known by the Celts as the 'Lady of the Mountains', it is associated with the cult of the goddess Brighid and for centuries has been thought by country people to be an oracular tree. It is for this reason that many women in ancient times wished their spinning wheels to be made of rowan. The base of the rowan-berry bears the pentagram mark, so these fruits were placed as protective sentinels at windows and doors on Hallowe'en.

Acorns, rattling about in their cups this month, were collected to keep in pockets. This charm of Druid origin was said to ward off ageing as long as the acorn remained smooth and glossy. Falling leaves were also caught mid-flight and preserved, both for decoration and as a folk prophylactic amulet against catching cold.

Spiders, being considered magic creatures, were sometimes used in desperation medicines for agues and ailments that would not shift. *The Fairfax Household Book* of the late seventeenth and early eighteenth centuries just recommends swallowing the web with nutmeg, pepper and rum, but an old English country remedy of the same period involved consuming a whole spider pressed inside a raisin!

A decoction of thyme was said to enable one to see the fairies; certainly served hot with honey it was good for a cough. Country people said of this medicine-chest staple:

Make thyme in time, while thyme lasts.
All time's no time, when time's past.

Ivy was also used in medicines, both topical and internal (French countrywomen still make anti-rheumatism tea from chopped ivy leaves and elder-bark), as well as to clean grease-spots from clothes. In *Grandmother's Secrets* (1973), Jean Palaiseul says, 'In many regions, particularly Italy, mothers used to plait caps of ivy for their infants, to reduce inflammation when their heads were covered with impetigo.'

* * *

Cleaning the dairy, larder and animal shelters was the pre-winter priority. Other October tasks included making baskets from clematis, bramble, jasmine, periwinkle, lilac or dogwood runners or suckers, as well as spinning (associated with the Greek spinning goddess of fates, Clotho), wool-carding, darning, smocking, mending and knitting (in early times done with needles made from the spindle-tree). Most women possessed not only a rag-bag and a button-bag, put also a piece-bag, where the best fragments of material would be stored for patchwork quilting.

Even when they finally had a chance to sit down and have a cup of tea, this relaxation interlude was sometimes used for divinatory purposes. One or more leaves floating on the surface of the beverage was taken to indicate that a visitor or visitors were shortly to arrive. Usually China tea was used for leaf-reading, and the enquirer after the future drank all the liquid until there was just over a teaspoon left. Traditionally the cup was held in the left hand, and gently swirled in a circular, anti-clockwise manner. At this point it was important for the enquirer to concentrate on the life-questions she wished answered, then to gently tip away the remaining liquid to see if the leaves had formed into shapes of good omen, such as horseshoes, acorns or anchors; or signs of negative portent such as bats, daggers or ravens.

Palm reading was also a popular cottage craft much practised by groups of women gathered together on all-female social occasions. Sometimes crystal-gazing also came into play: many women simply used bowls or glasses of water to conjure forth their visions (while sucking or gnawing nutmegs – containing narcotic oils. If they were wealthy they might instead use scrying-globes made of rock-crystal or beryl. The ritual of looking into a reflective surface for purposes of augury and entry into the world of the spirits has its origins in the ancient Roman mystic cult of the Specularii, or mirror-diviners, whose mirrors were a symbol of Venus. Earlier still, in ancient Egypt the goddess Hathor's symbol, the ankh, represented a mirror.

Gemstones were also universally used throughout medieval Europe for both healing and oracular purposes. Moonstones, known in France as *pierres de la lune*, have always been associated with lunar deities and thus with women and were in times of old held in the mouth under a waning moon to stimulate prophetic visions. In the Middle Ages, the cloudiness or clarity of the stone was thought to be an accurate barometer of the owner's health and well-being.

Hallowe'en was the night when women used mirrors in an assortment of rites designed to reveal to them the identity of their future suitor/s. (In later years, at least, these activities must have been undertaken with a certain degree of levity!) One involved walking backwards out of doors wearing seven petticoats, looking into a mirror by moonlight. Another required the seeker to brush her hair by candlelight, gazing into the mirror in a trance-like state. Looking over one's shoulder was forbidden, in case Old Nick took advantage of the moment of lapsed concentration to loom large in the mirror! After all this occult over-excitement it would be no surprise if sleep were a difficulty. Slippers or shoes were carefully placed upside down

beside the bed to ward off night cramps, and crackly herbal sleep
pillows or soporific scented bags of dried summer flowers to put
inside pillowcases were employed with nervous enthusiasm.

A Bag To Smell Unto, Or To Cause One To Sleep

Take drie Rose leaves, keep them close in a glasse which will
keep them sweet, then take powder of Mints, powder of
Cloves in a grosse powder. Put the same to the Rose leaves,
then put all these together in a bag, and take that to bed with
you, and it will cause you to sleepe, and it is good too smell
unto at other times.

Ram's Little Dodoen, 1606

Even using a soft feather mattress and pillows whose surface
had newly been made feather-proof by rubbing a candle-stub
over the ticking, nightmares and vivid dreams could not be
completely quelled in this supernatural month. (In ancient
Egypt the goddess of truth and justice, Maat, is symbolised by a
feather hieroglyph.) In Greece and Rome dreams were believed
to be direct messages from the gods. Many women in the past
kept dream diaries, updated as soon as they awoke. Then, as
today, women used this scrambled information so that they
could interpret prophetic hidden personal messages, imageries
and mythologies from the world of sleep: the Underworld
vestibule known to the ancients as the Grove of
Persephone/Prosperine.

> In a dark tree there hides
> A bough, all golden, leaf and plant stem,
> Sacred to Proserpine. This all the grove
> Protects, and shadows cover it with darkness.
>
> Virgil

November

For now we see through a glass, darkly:

I Corinthians, xiii, II

Dry up your tears, and stick your rosemary
On this fair corse.

Romeo and Juliet, William Shakespeare

Upon a Lady That Died in Childbed, and
Left a Daughter Behind Her
As gillyflowers do but stay
To blow, and seed, and so away;
So you, sweet lady (sweet as May),
The garden's glory, lived awhile
To lend the world your scent and smile.
But when your own fair print was set
Once in a virgin flosculet
(Sweet as yourself, and newly-blown),
To give that life, resigned your own:
But so, as still the mother's power
Lives in the pretty lady flower.

Robert Herrick

O, thought I! What a beautiful thing God has made winter to be, by stripping the trees and letting us see their shapes and forms. What a freedom does it seem to give to the storms.

Dorothy Wordsworth quoted in
The English Landscape in Picture, Prose and Poetry,
edited by Kathleen Conyngham Greene, 1932

Marriage, birth or buryin',
News across the seas,
All our sad, or merryin'
You must tell the bees.

Anon

Helen takes honey, milk and wine to Clytemnestra's tomb to pour in mingled streams.

Orestes, Euripedes

Black bat, bear away,
Come again another day.

Traditional

The proper way of life for a widowed woman is to be sober and do without unnecessary knick-knacks.

The Treasure of the City of Ladies, Christine de Pisan, 1405

ll Hallow's Day and All Saints' Day on November 1 and 2 commemorate Christian saints and martyrs and the souls of the departed, an echo of the Celtic Feast of the Dead which also took place at this time. In ancient Egypt the mummified dead were entombed wearing the scarab sign of immortality and the pale blue precious stones of Hathor, Lady of the Turquoise. The underside of the lid of the sarcophagi (made of cypress wood in the case of queens and priestesses) was often painted with images of the winged goddess of the skies, Nut. Hieroglyphs of the afterlife adorned the walls of many tombs – sometimes with images of the heart of the deceased being weighed against the goddess of truth, Maat, or of the soul being welcomed to the afterworld by the goddesses Isis and her twin sister Nephthys.

Flowers and herbs have been linked to rituals for the dead for ages. A 3000-year-old funerary flower has been found in the tomb of Tutankhamun. Rosemary was one of the funerary wreath and incense herbs used by the Egyptians and the Greeks, who also strewed iris blossoms and parsley on the graves of women. The Romans also used incense (Nero used cinnamon for the pyre of Poppaea) and believed that the ghosts of the dead inhabited beans – and that to dream of beans or bean flowers presaged bad luck, a superstition which has lingered in modern Europe. Rosemary was still being used in England as an aromatic, antiseptic and preservative funerary herb in Shakespearean times. Its symbolic value, we know from Ophelia's interment in *Hamlet*, was for 'remembrance'.

As well as being participants in the magical birth process, women have long been especially involved with the final rite of passage. In Europe women have kept an eagle eye, in this often bitterly cold month, on omens relating to impending extinction: flowers with prematurely drooping heads, mysterious knockings on the window pane, candles guttering in the shape of a winding sheet, coffin-shaped coals flying out of the fire, pictures falling from the wall, birds flying down the chimney, death-watch beetles clicking, scissors falling point down, etc.

Strict rules were observed at a death bedside: the dying person must never be left in the dark or unaccompanied by the living, for example, and windows and doors must be unlocked to allow the departing soul easy exit. The bed of the person 'in limbo' had to be placed in the same direction as the ceiling beams and floorboards so the devil could not steal their soul.

When death had actually taken place, female family members would cover any mirrors in the house with a cloth, in case the spirit of the deceased was still lurking about and became ensnared in the reflection. Clocks were stopped until after the funeral. The body would be washed, and a dish of salt, both an anti-evil condiment and a symbol of eternity, would be left on or near the body. Mourners often walked round the body clockwise with lighted candles ('sained'). Since the remote past, the eyes of a dead person have been closed and covered with a silver coin – a lunar symbol of resurrection.

Women's role worldwide as vocal mourners wailing, ululating and keening on the way to and by the graveside (sometimes as 'professional' paid lamenters) is well documented, but in England up until Victorian times it was also common for women to act as pall-bearers for women, small children and babies. Before the middle of the eighteenth century in Europe coffins were rare – most people were shrouded in a blanket, or in the case of poor women, a red flannel petticoat. Young women carried the white-draped pall (body-pallet) or coffin of a departed female contemporary, and hung up a complex herbal or paper floral tribute to her – called a Maiden's Garland – in the church. Women who died in childbirth also had their coffins draped in white cloth, a residual folk memory perhaps of the times when the white robes of women who died in this way were dedicated to Artemis on her altar.

Until the advent of Victorian grave-robbing mania it was quite usual for a few meaningful personal possessions to be wrapped in women's shrouds as votive offerings, just as Celtic women in ancient times were laid to rest with their burnished hand-mirrors, as soul-carriers. In her poem 'Last Words', Sylvia Plath asks to be buried with her rouge pots and cooking pots, and begs for a sarcophagus with 'a face on it/Round as the moon, to stare up.'

The rose has been a floral grief emblem on the grave since Roman times. In some places white blooms are used for children and unmarried women; in France they are mingled with orange-blossom. In Germany scented pinks have been used traditionally on children's graves.

The Periwinkle

The flower is called by the Italians 'The Flower of Death', from the ancient custom of making it into garlands to place on the biers of dead children.

A Modern Herbal, Mrs Grieve, 1931

It was considered most important for the family bees to be informed of the death in the household, and for them to be formally invited to the funeral. Black ribbon was sometimes tied round the hive and also attached to the favourite garden plants and trees of the departed. In some parts of the British Isles in the medieval period, teardrop shapes were painted on windows and doors as a sign of mourning. Victorian women wore mourning rings made of the plaited hair of the late beloved, and the rich among them wore cult 'jewellery of grief' such as amethysts, pearls ('tears of sorrow') and jet. The latter hard coal substance was once the emblem of Cybele, Greek earth goddess of caves and the underworld.

* * *

November, although associated with the Grim Reaper, also, conversely, has connotations of feasting and jollity. In the Saxon calendar it was called both Wintmonat (the windy month) and Blotmonat (the bloody month) because of the annual slaughter of all livestock which could not be fed through the winter. This 'festive' culling (which always took place when there was a waxing moon) and the subsequent curing of meat traditionally took place around the medieval feast of St Martin, which fell on 11 November. Absolutely nothing was wasted: hams were put in brine and/or sugar, blood puddings were made and highly seasoned sausage was hooked up in the chimney to cure. Fresh lard – made from pigs fattened in orchards, and subsequently flavoured with rosemary or lavender – was a popular lunchbox bread spread in the English Cotswolds when sowing had to be undertaken by hand in the frosty fields. Also popular was a thick, savoury barley stew called frumenty, often eaten cold:

> Wife, sometime this weeke, if the weather hold cleere,
> An end to wheat sowing we make for this yeere,
> Remember you therefore, though I do it not,
> The seede Cake, the Pasties, and Furmentie pot.
> *Five Hundredth Pointes of Good Husbandrie*,
> Thomas Tusser, 1573

In Mediterranean areas November heralded, as well as seed-sowing, the start of the olive harvest. In Provence women kept the paste left over after the olive-fruit pressings to mix with lavender to make a large batch of aromatic soap for laundry and personal use (to massage into their nails, for example, or to add to bath water or make a rich mayonnaise to treat dry hair).

* * *

This month is crammed with saints' days. 17 November is dedicated to St Hilda, who in 657AD founded a double monastery for men and women at Whitby in Yorkshire:

> She taught the observance of righteousness, mercy, purity
> and other virtues, but especially of peace and charity.
> The Venerable Bede

22 November is sacred to St Cecilia, a Roman maiden who achieved martyrdom during the reign of Marcus Aurelius. She was chosen as patron of the guild of musicians in London in the Middle Ages:

> And whil the organs maden melodie
> To God allone in harte thus sang she.
> > Cecilia, described in the *Second Nun's Tale*,
> > Geoffrey Chaucer

Taking a leaf out of Cecilia's book, in medieval Germany Hildegarde of Bingen wrote her 77 songs called *The Symphony of Harmony of Celestial Revelations*. They include 'O Ecclesia', which personified the church as a woman, 'The Bride of Christ'.

On 25 November in England the feast of St Catherine (known familiarly as 'Cattern') was celebrated with great gusto. This Alexandrian intellectual, said to have died for her faith on a spiked wheel in the fourth century, became the patron saint of spinners, women students and young unmarried women. Catherine's wheel was also symbolic of the spiritual energy field known as the etheric body.

On St Catherine's Eve female followers of the saint prepared a celebratory Cattern Bowl, which involved roasting apples in the fire and tossing the hot apple pulp into a large bowl brimming with cider spiced with cinnamon quills. Early the next day they made delicate wheel-shaped Cattern cakes or pies flavoured with cinnamon, caraway seeds and almonds.

> Rise, maidens rise
> Bake your Cattern pies
> > Traditional

St Catherine is also patron of lace-makers because of confusion between the saint and Queen Katherine of Aragon, who, hearing that Bedfordshire lace-makers were starving through lack of work, burned all her lace and ordered a new supply. On St Catherine's Day lace-makers would have a party, the highlight of which was a ceremony which involved leaping over a lighted candlestick. The girls who managed not to put out the flame with their swishing skirts were assured of good luck for the following year.

> Kit be nimble, Kit be quick
> Kit jump o'er the candlestick.
>
> Nursery rhyme

* * *

Advent Sunday, four Sundays before Christmas, was always known as 'Stir-Up Sunday', from the old custom of ceremonially making the Christmas pudding on this day. The name came from the Collect for the Sunday before Advent, which resounds:

> Stir up we beseech Thee, O Lord,
> The wills of thy faithful people.

All the family had to take a turn in stirring the rich mixture sunwise while making a wish. Then the mother, or most senior female household member, would hide a coin, a thimble and a ring in the pudding, symbolising wealth, a single life, and an impending love-match. The pudding has its origins in a magical meat-and-wheat fertility porridge eaten at this time by ancient Britons in honour of the sun god.

> Pour the brandy liberally.
> Stir and wish, then three times three.
>
> *Stirring the Pudding*, Eleanor Farjeon

Scandinavian and German Advent features highly decorated aniseed biscuits made to be eaten each Sunday when the Advent candle is lit to herald the birth of the Christ child. The candle itself is sometimes held firm in a star-shaped honey and gingerbread biscuit. In Germany the *Zopf*, or braided loaf, used

170

to be eaten only on or around All Hallow's Day (*Allerseelen*), to commemorate – according to Sarah Kelly's *Festive Baking in Austria, Germany and Switzerland* – 'the days when a warrior's wife would have her plait cut off before joining him in the grave'.

* * *

In addition to the meat-curing and cooking (jellies and purées from rose-hips and other hedgerow berries such as sea buckthorn were made now), family ailments had to be physicked particularly well in this dangerous month of grey mist and dull curtains of rain and icy sleet.

A good cook is half a physician.

Herbal, Nicholas Culpeper, 1653

Poultices for boils and aches were made from roasted onions filled with frankincense; children with weak chests were rubbed down with goose fat; and cinnamon in milk was a standby for anyone with an upset stomach (in France they prefer their cinnamon in wine!) A clove of honey-drenched garlic was thought just the ticket for ear-ache, and sore throats were treated to frequent spoonfuls of hot blackberry jam. Old people wrapped cabbage leaves around their swollen rheumatic joints. Infusions of October's hypericum (also known as holy herb) flowers would now be sitting on most country windowsills infusing, in readiness for being used against asthma, bronchitis, and gynaecological problems.

An old English country cure for chilblains was to rinse them in a chamber-pot of urine first thing in the morning; or to run about barefoot in the snow, after which a mashed turnip poultice might be applied. Pepper was sometimes sprinkled in socks 'to warm the feet', but really chilled extremities called for a steaming footbath with mustard dissolved in it.

Problems with the 'Surroundings of the Heart', claimed the *Ladies Dispensatory* of 1651, could be vanquished with 'The

Smell of Cowcumbers', and hot flushes were treated with teas made of infusions of sage, hawthorn and motherwort, and, in the case of American pioneer women, pumpkin. Thomas Dawson's *The Good Housewife's Jewel* (1596) recommended that those suffering from 'Sinews Broken in Two' might benefit from a slippery medicine whose recipe begins: 'Take worms while they be nice, and look that they depart not ...' More appetisingly, those who had partaken too liberally or too fast of November's food bounty and were consequently suffering from indigestion, heartburn or other related ills might well take:

A Powder To Stop Hiccups in Man, Woman or Child
Put as much Dill-seed, finely powdered, as will lie on a shilling, into two spoonsful of syrup of Black Cherries, and take it presently.

The Country Housewife, 1753

Magical help was invoked if country cures proved ineffective – amulets bearing the old Hebrew charm ABRACADABRA were sometimes worn hanging from a black ribbon, alongside a dried rabbit's foot, a necklace of blue beads or a snakeskin garter. It was considered a very bad omen in folk belief if the family cat decided to leave the house while someone was ill, and a very bad move to refuse to feed a stray cat – cats were once sacred to Diana and to Freya, whose chariot they pulled through the sky. Rubbing an infected eye with the tail of a black cat was a popular folk remedy throughout medieval Europe.

This being the season of chapped lips and dry skin, women turned to the 'beauty' section of their stillroom shelves, or to the larder. French women combated winter skin problems with face-masks of olive oil and mashed cauliflower, or starch and rosewater. Upper-class English girls, pale from being kept indoors, pinched their cheeks to give themselves a 'healthy glow'. Some resorted to artifice, such as:

A Cosmetick Wonderful to Make a Pleasing Ruddy Complexion
Take Madder, Myrrh, Saffron, Frankincense of each alike,
bruise and steep all on White-wine, with which anoint the
face going to bed, and in the morning wash it off, and the skin
will have a gallant, pleasing blush.

Polygraphices, W Salmon Esq, seventeenth century

A winter facial wash utilising aromatic juniper berries or the
clove-scented roots of herb bennet were recommended ·in
seventeenth-century English household books, and if the object
of one's affections did not respond to such improvements, there
were always magical aphrodisiac allurements to be made.
'Kissing comfits and snow eringoes' are recommended love-aids
in Shakespeare's *The Merry Wives of Windsor*; the eringoe is a
sweetmeat made of the sea holly root.

A more blunt and independent invitation to the desired one
was the giving of a piece of 'cockle bread' – a piece of dough
pressed into shape around the vulva, then baked. Not for
nothing did *The Old Bridal Calendar* suggest that the November
bride was saucy: 'inclined to be lawless'.

* * *

Even at this time of year there was work in the garden: taking
hardwood cuttings, tree-pruning, bringing tender herbs indoors to
overwinter, planting garlic, sowing angelica seeds, digging and
mulching the vegetable plot hotbeds for early carrots and radishes:

Every lady should be careful, when she has finished digging,
to have her spade dipped in water, and then wiped dry; after
which it should be hung up in some warm dry shed, or harness
room, to keep it free from rust.

Practical Instructions in Gardening for Ladies,
Mrs Jane Loudon, 1841

* * *

Keeping warm, however, was the main consideration in November – even the bees had to be kept cosy with straw or blankets round the hive. A good supply of firewood and kindling was of paramount importance, but throughout Europe the choosing and using of firewood was governed by strict folk laws. The wood from the tamarisk tree, which blooms in November, was taboo in Italy as a cursed wood which made 'neither fire nor ashes'. Holly, with its Druidic associations, was taboo firewood in England, along with water-divining hazel, magic rowan and elder, although impromptu bellows of hollow elder-stem were made.

Dried sun-yellow flowers of hypericum were burned on the fire to keep lightning away from the house, and dried rosemary to promote family harmony. Talismanic horse-brasses featuring the sun, moon and stars were polished to a brilliant shine on the fireplace beam.

> Elm she burns like the churchyard mould
> Even the very flames are cold.
> Birch and Pine-wood burn too fast –
> Blaze too bright and do not last.
> But Ash wet or Ash dry
> A Queen may warm her slippers by.
>
> Traditional English rhyme

December

Holly he hath berries as red as any rose,
The foresters and the hunters keep them from the does;
Ivy she hath berries as black as any sloe;
Then come the owls and eat them as they go.
Good ivy, we say – What birds hast thou?
Nought but an owlet crying How! How! How!

Some of the original words to the carol
'The Holly and the Ivy'

Dame get up and bake your pies,
Bake your pies, bake your pies.
Dame get up and bake your pies
On Christmas Day in the morning.

Traditional English song

Come, and if it lyke you
To dauncen, daunceth with us now.
And I, withoute tarrying,
Wente into the karolying.

Romaunt of the Rose, Geoffrey Chaucer

A December bride is graceful in person, fond of novelty, fascinating, but a spendthrift.

The Old Bridal Calendar

To Frost Holly-leaves, for Garnishing
Ingredients – *Sprigs of holly, oiled butter, coarsely powdered sugar.*
Mode – procure some nice sprigs of holly; pick the leaves from
the stalks, and wipe them with a clean cloth free from all
moisture; then place them on a dish near the fire, to get
thoroughly dry, but not too near to shrivel the leaves; dip
them into oiled butter, sprinkle over them some coarsely
powdered sugar, and dry them before the fire. They should be
kept in a dry place, as the least damp would spoil their
appearance.

The Book of Household Management,
Mrs Isabella Beeton, 1861

To Mull Wine
Boil the quantity you choose, of cinnamon, nutmeg grated,
cloves or mace, in a quarter pint of water; add a pint of port,
and sugar to taste, boil it up, and serve, with thin slices of
toast.

The English Housekeeper, Ann Cobbett, 1851

There were delicious remedies for bad colds. We had linseed
tea, a thick liquor made from linseed, flavoured with sticks of
black liquorice. We loved to sip this smooth, sweet drink,
which was not dissimilar from a cure we gave the cows for
colds. No wonder the cattle supped it eagerly! We had thin
gruel, sweetened with honey, and hot caudles and treacle
possets. In the night we drank blackcurrant tea.

Country Things, Alison Uttley, 1946

Three ladies came from the east,
One with fire, and two with frost.
Out with fire, in with frost.

West Country charm for scalds and burns

ntil the Reformation, English women and girls carried home-made shrines containing holly, ivy and images of the Virgin Mary and Holy Child (known as M'Lady, or Milly, boxes) from house to house in the Advent season. It was believed that bad luck would befall anyone who did not give a bright new coin to the frost-defying Millies and receive a leaf of life-symbolic greenery from the display in return. Brightness and luck-enhancing also featured in the ritual of eating food by the light of the Advent candle common throughout icy northern Europe and Scandinavia in the run-up to the curious hybrid Christian/pagan festival of Christmas. Often these illuminations were enormous and were made from wax candlestubs saved up all year by housewives, incorporating the remains of the previous year's Christmas candle in the centre.

On St Barbara's Day on 4 December, in the north of England, an old wives' prophylactic against winter chills was to eat cress – known as St Barbara's Cress – in great quantities. Barbara, a deity associated with thunder and lightning, was placated by offerings from French peasants when they planted wheat on her day. 8 December commemorated the Feast of the Immaculate Conception of the Virgin Mary, when according to Christian doctrine the patron saint of housewives, St Anne, partheno-genetically conceived Mary – who is still addressed by such ancient creator epithets as Lady of the Universe and Empress of Heaven.

13 December was St Lucy's Day, honouring a fourth-century martyr from Syracuse who legendarily spurned an indefatigable suitor besotted by her beautiful eyes by sending the orbs to him on a plate! As a result of her blind devotions, Lucia's sight was miraculously restored, thus making her a favourite with the ophthalmically challenged. In Sweden Lucia is very important as a symbol of the rebirth of light in the season of darkness.

Village girls in rural areas who are chosen as representatives of the saint parade about wearing crowns of lighted candles and carrying star-wands. *The Fairfax Household Book* in England in the seventeenth and eighteenth centuries recommended curing sore eyes with 'red wine, rose water and woman's milk'.

* * *

Minced-pie season traditionally begins in England on 16 December. These Christmas edibles were originally made of minced lamb flavoured with sugar and 'Holy Land' spices, and the pastry case was shaped either oblong or oval to represent Christ's manger, complete with pastry baby on the lid. Similarly in Germany, the aromatic white cake *stollen* is an image of the Christ-child in swaddling-bands. Throughout the Advent season in Germany Christmas fairs – *Weinachtmarkts* – are held in marketplaces, selling spicy, honeyed Advent biscuits in a huge array of elaborate patterns and shapes created from carved wooden moulds that used to be part of young women's dowries. In Provence in southern France, women make traditional flat cakes called *fougasso*, woven like wicker cradles from dough made with olive oil.

Ghosts, wraiths, witches and goblins were said to lurk throughout this pagan month of the Long Night Moon, but traditionally in the British Isles they came out and disported themselves on St Thomas' Eve, 20 December. Young women wishing to dream vividly of their future love life stuck pins in a raw onion (associated with magic by the ancient Egyptians, Greeks and Romans), saying: 'Good St Thomas, do me right/And let my true love come tonight' – thereafter putting the prickly onion, wrapped in a handkerchief, under their pillow. If no dream were forthcoming, violet and rose-petal tea was sometimes taken with honey, 'For A Sad Heart'. On St Thomas' Day itself, the date of the Winter Solstice, poor women went to the local woman farmer to be given flour with which to make Yule bread, and wheat for the festive frumenty, a savoury porridge thickened at Christmas with dried fruit. It was considered good luck in needy households to leave a spoonful of frumenty in a saucer on the doorstep for the fairies.

* * *

Medieval women brought decorative greenery – holly, ivy, rosemary, laurel and bay – into the house on Christmas Eve, and not before. The use of resurrection-symbolic evergreens at a midwinter festival dates back to the Roman light and fire feast of Saturnalia, during which the Birthday of the Unconquered Sun was celebrated. This seven-day fest ran into the New Year rites of Kalends. In medieval Christmas mythology rosemary was associated with the Virgin Mary, who dried her baby's wrapping on a bush of the plant.

In England the mystic fertility emblem mistletoe – 'The Golden Bough', once cut by Druidic priests and priestesses with a golden sickle during the Winter Solstice – was brought indoors from the apple orchards or woods to incorporate into a vast 'Kissing Bough'. This magnificent emblem comprised a wooden or woven osier frame bedecked with greenery (mistletoe at the centre), ribbons, nuts, and cloth decorations, hanging from the main ceiling beam of a house. As part of this veneration of vegetation, no one could refuse a kiss while berries remained on the mistletoe plant. Childless women wore necklaces and bracelets of the white berries during the 12 days of Christmas from the Nativity to Epiphany as a conception insurance policy and to ward off supernatural sprites.

Ivy, in plant mythology a 'feminine' entity, had its own fertility cult and was made into bridal crowns for Saxon betrothals. The spiral nature of its evergreen growth made it a symbol of life and rebirth. Ivy clinging to the wall of a house was thought to be a propitious omen that would protect it from malign influence, while on a more prosaic level its leaves, simmered in wine, were used to cure drunkenness and hangovers. Its tiny winter flowers were a useful nectar-source for the family bees.

Holly berries, because of their magical red colour, were threaded together for garlands over the hearth and were also frequently used powdered as a tonic medicine for humans and animals. The wood from their branches was sometimes kept to make special household objects like spoons, teapot lids or door-handles, but to wantonly burn the holly (or holy-tree) as firewood was very illomened, unless it was saved to cook pancakes on Shrove Tuesday or to ignite next year's Christmas pudding.

The fir 'Christmas tree' as we know it had its origins in Germany, but the concept of a decorated tree brought inside for a festival dates back as far as 2000 BC, when an evergreen tree hung with offerings of nuts, sweetmeats, jewellery and gaily coloured trinkets was offered at the altar of the Mesopotamian virgin-mother goddess Astarte to give thanks for the birth of her divine child, the Sun.

On Christmas Eve the Yule log (*juul* is Saxon/Norse for 'light'), fuel for the return of the sun, was dragged in from the woods, according to some sources with a girl enthroned upon it representing the spirit of the tree. The log was usually oak or ash, the wood of the pagan Scandinavian world-tree Yggdrasil upon whose boughs heaven was thought to have rested. The Yule log – or ashen faggot, as it was known when it consisted of a vast bundle of thin branches tied with thin, supple ash branches – was always kindled with a fragment of the previous year's log – a custom common to most European countries. Tending it carefully was essential, as it was not allowed to go out for the 12 days of Christmas. Only cleansed hands were allowed to participate in the sacred Yule fire-tending rituals:

> Unwash't hands, ye maidens know,
> Dead the fire, though ye blow!
> *Discovering Christmas Customs and Folklore*,
> Margaret Baker, 1968

* * *

Before round-the-fire merriment could begin – the eating of Sugar Jumball biscuits, the playing of games, and the copious drinking of hot spiced wine and beer (young women were advised to be literally and metaphorically well-girdled against the lust-inducing properties of cinnamon and cloves) – the housewife had to feed the family bees, for on Christmas Eve at midnight they were said to hum the 100th psalm.

> Go look to thy bees, if the hive be too light
> Set honey and water, with rosemary dight [decked].
> Which set a dish full of sticks in the hive
> From danger of famine will save them alive.
> > *Five Hundredth Pointes of Good Husbandrie*,
> > Thomas Tusser, 1573

Other animals and poultry also got a mixture of grain and lard known as the Christmas sheaf, which sustained them through this special night when it was believed they talked amongst themselves.

In many parts of Europe one of the first things a woman did as it grew dark on Christmas Eve was to light a candle in the kitchen window. It was considered important for good luck in the forthcoming year that it was still alight when she returned from midnight Mass.

In Cornwall on this night, women traditionally made Stargazey Pie, a large shortcrust pastry construction from which pilchards' heads 'gazed' at the sky. Venetian women meanwhile busied themselves creating a complex tower of *Torta de Lasagne*: pasta and sauce layers enlivened with the seasonal addition of pine-nuts, raisins, currants and orange-peel. In southern France it is traditional not to eat until after midnight Mass, when spiced wine is served with 13 desserts, representing Jesus and his disciples.

In medieval England it was usual for those who went from door-to-door carol-singing (carols were originally secular winter folk-ballads with dancing) to be given special marzipan/marchpane cakes (almonds are mentioned in the Scriptures), crimson biscuits coloured with beetroot, Yule figures made of gingerbread, and posset, sugared ale with milk and eggs. As well as carol-singers, there were visits from Mummers performing ancient folk-plays (featuring the antics of, among others, Punch and Judy), handbell-ringers and Wassailers (from the Anglo-Saxon *Waeshael* – 'good health') carrying large wooden bowls of punch with which to drink the health of the householders:

> O come down, young maid with your silver-headed pin,
> Open the door and let us all come in.
> Then you will see how very merry we can be.
> For it is your jolly Wassail! And, it is ours!
>
> 'Song of the Wassailers', West Country

Bread baked on Christmas Day itself was believed to have magical curative properties, so a number of loaves were put by to be powdered for use as a medicine later in the year. In the seventeenth century dolls made on Christmas Eve from pastry scraps were set in decorated boxes and given to small children on Christmas morning along with their symbolic presents of an apple, an orange, a new penny, a lump of coal and some salt. In the Elizabethan era it was common among gentlemen of rank to give ladies a Christmas present of an opal, the stone of the Roman goddess of plenty Ops, or Ceres, who had her own festival within the Saturnalia, or to give a silvered or gilded nutmeg:

> I had a little nut-tree, nothing would it bear
> But a silver nutmeg and a golden pear.
>
> Nursery rhyme

Christmas pudding was originally a meat porridge with prunes and raisins – it didn't become ball-shaped and completely non-savoury until Victorian times.

There were many other imaginative alternatives:

To Make a Dish of Snow

Take a pottle of sweet thick cream, and the white of eyght Egs, and beat them altogether, with a spoone, then put them into your cream with a dishfull of Rosewater, and a dishfull of Sugar withall ... take a platter and sette an Apple in the midst of it, stick a thicke bush of Rosemary in the Apple. Then cast your snow upon the Rosemary and fill your platter therewith.

A Book of Cookerie, Anon, 1594

For women farmers Boxing Day was not free from baking. It was traditional on this day – named after the almsboxes for the poor which were kept in the church and opened now for distribution – for them to make vast pies from Christmas leftovers to be given out to the needy of the parish.

* * *

Despite the hectic work to be done in the kitchen creating festive food – tea-creams, warden [pear] pies, syllabubs, toffees, baked apple-snows, etc. – and the overseeing of the Yule fire, women kept the house as clean as they could, for on Christmas Eve in particular, ghosts were abroad and might visit their old homes to see that standards were being adhered to. It was a strict rule that though homes had to be well swept, besom brooms must not be manufactured during the 12 days of the Christmas period, or bad luck would come to their owners during the coming year.

It was considered particularly ill-favoured to do any washing or housework on December 28 in rural England. Known as 'Childermas', this day commemorated the slaughter by Herod of the Hebrew babies – the 'Holy Innocents'. Gentlewomen therefore battled with the midwinter miasmas of unwashed clothes and body odours by heaping dishes high with pungently perfumed pomanders made of oranges and lemons stuck with cloves and rolled in orris root and cinnamon powders. They also burned resins and aromatic roots like angelica – 'the happy counterbane' and 'the root of the Holy Ghost' – that also protected homes from sorcery on little chafing dishes by the fire:

To Perfume a House, and Purify The Air
Take a root of Angelica, dry it in an oven, or before the fire,
then bruise it well and infuse it 4 or 5 days in White Wine
Vinegar. When you use it, lay it upon a brick made hot, and
repeat the operation several times.

The Toilet of Flora, PJ Buchoz, 1784

There was also work to do in the animal-pens: dung-gathering
for drying for fuel, for example. And in the bleak garden in
December: digging and mulching the ground, sowing peas and
beans, as well as harvesting cabbages and carrots. The flower,
herb and vegetable seeds garnered over the last year had to be
checked for mildew and methodically sorted in order of spring
sowing.

From the store-room, onions, horseradish and garlic were
much employed against an enormous number of winter ailments,
although the latter, even after caraway or cardamon comfits, was
not smiled on for those heading for the Kissing Bough:

We absolutely forbid it into our Salleting, by reasons of its
intolerable Rankness ... 'tis not for Ladies Palats, nor those
who court them.

Diarist John Evelyn, speaking of garlic in
the seventeenth century

The stillroom dried herb store and apothecary cabinet was
also much raided now for remedies, whether it be a treacle-and-
elderflower medicine against the plague, powdered spindle-
berries for head-lice, woodlice in beer for a cough, beeswax and
pine-resin for boils, leeks stewed in sea-water for 'hardness of the
womb', dove's dung and frankincense for lung ailments, or
tincture of myrrh for anaemia in young girls. Mistletoe, or 'Cure-
All', was much employed, as were the leaves of the sweet bay,
once used to crown Delphic priestesses and latterly in remedies
for the Christmas maladies of hysteria and colic, bought on by
stress and overeating.

The contents of the many tiny drawers of the apothecary cabinet also came in useful for festive season beauty aids, but there were those who chose more exotic and difficult-to-come-by ingredients:

For Heat or Pimples in the Face

Take the liverwort that groweth in the well, stamp and strain it and put the juice into a cream, and so annoint your face as long as you will and it will help you. Proved.

The Queen's Closet Opened, WM, 1655

Others relied on the kitchen for help with a softly gleaming Christmas smile:

To mak a salve for the lips

Take two ounces of whit bees wax: and slice it thin: then melt it over the fire with two ounces of sugar Candi: and when you see it is well incorporated take it off the fire and let it stand till it be cold: then set the skillet on the fire agane: till the bottom is warm and so turn it out.

Recipes and Remedies 1669–1712, Jane Mosley

Select Bibliography

Achterberg, Jeanne, *Woman as Healer*, Shambala, Massachusetts, 1990

Acton, Eliza, *Modern Cookery for Private Families*, 1845

Addison, Josephine, *The Illustrated Plant Lore*, Guild Publishing, 1985

Anon, *A Book of Cookerie*, 1594

Anon, *A Book of Fruits and Flowers*, 1653, published in facsimile, Prospect Books, 1984

Anon, *The Good Huswife's Handmaid*, 1597

Baker, Margaret, *Discovering Christmas Customs and Folklore*, Shire, 1968, reprinted Shire, 1992

—*Discovering the Folklore of Plants*, 1928, reprinted Shire, 1996

—*Folklore and Customs in Rural England*, David & Charles, 1974

Balston, Thomas and Geoffrey Bles, eds, *The Housekeeping Book of Susanna Whatman 1776–1800*, 1956

Bancke's Herbal, 1525

Baring, Anne and Jules Cashford, *The Myth of the Goddess*, Arkana, 1991

Beeton, Isabella, *The Book of Household Management*, 1861

Beith, Mary, *Healing Threads – Traditional Medicines of the Highlands and Islands*, Polygon, 1995

Boland, Maureen and Bridget, *Old Wives' Lore for Gardeners*, The Bodley Head, 1976

Boorde, Dr Andrew, *The Dietary of Health*, 1547

Buchoz, PJ, *The Toilet of Flora*, 1784

Chamber, R, *The Book of Days*, 1864/1866

Clare, John, *The Shepherd's Calendar*, 1827

Coates, Doris, *Tuppeny Rice and Treacle: Cottage Housekeeping 1900–20*, David & Charles, 1975

Cobbett, Ann, *The English Housekeeper*, 1851

Cockayne, TO, *Leechdoms, Wortcunning and Starcraft of Early England*, 1864

Cosman, Madeleine Pelner, *Mediaeval Holidays and Festivals*, Piatkus, 1996

The Country Housewife, 1753

Craig, Elizabeth, *Enquire Within*, 1948

Culpeper, Nicholas, *Herbal*, 1653

Davidson, Caroline, *A Woman's Work Is Never Done – A History of Housework in the British Isles 1650–1950*, Chatto & Windus, 1982

Dawson, Thomas, *The Good Housewife's Jewel*, 1596

De Salis, Mrs, *Household Wrinkles*, 1890

Dick, Diana, *Yesterday's Babies*, The Bodley Head, 1987

Domestic Cookery, 1834

Duby, Georges and Michelle Perrot, general eds, *A History of Women: From Ancient Goddesses to Christian Saints*, Belknap Harvard, Massachusetts, 1993

—*Silences of the Middle Ages*, Belknap Harvard, Massachusetts, 1993

—*Renaissance and Enlightenment Paradoxes*, Belknap Harvard, Massachusetts, 1993

Estienne, C and J Liebault, *Maison Rustique*, 1570, translated by R Surflet, 1600

Evelyn, John, *A Discourse of Sallets*, 1699

Fairfax Household Book, seventeenth/eighteenth centuries

Fernie, WT, *Herbal Simples*, 1910

Fitzherbert, Sir Anthony, *Boke of Husbandry*, 1525

Gerard, John, *Herbal*, 1597

Glasse, Mrs Hannah, *The Art of Cookery Made Plain and Easy*, 1747

Grieve, Mrs (Maud), *A Modern Herbal*, Cape, 1931

Groundes-Peace, Zara, *Mrs Groundes-Peace's Old Cookery Notebook*, Robin Howe, ed, David & Charles, 1971

Mrs Harrington's Book, eighteenth century

Hartley, Dorothy, *The Countryman's England*, Batsford, 1935

—*Food in England*, Macdonald & Co, 1954, reprinted Little, Brown, 1996

Hazlitt, W, *Dictionary of Faiths and Folklore*, Reeves and Turner, 1905

Holden, Edith, *The Country Diary of an Edwardian Lady*, 1906, reprinted Michael Joseph, 1977

Hone, W, *Hone's Everyday Book*, 1802

Hufton, Olwen, *The Prospect Before Her – A History of Women in Western Europe*, Volume I, HarperCollins, 1995

Jacob, Dorothy, *A Witch's Guide to Gardening*, Elek, 1964

Jekyll, Gertrude, *Children and Gardens*, no date

Jones, Julia and Barbara Dear, *Cattern Cakes and Lace*, Dorling Kindersley, 1987

JW, *The Art of Gardening*, 1677

Kelly, Sarah, *Festive Baking in Austria, Germany and Switzerland*, Penguin, 1985

Labarge, Margaret Wade, *A Small Sound of the Trumpet – Women in Mediaeval Life*, Hamish Hamilton, 1990

Laurence, Anne, *Women in England 1500–1760: A Social History*, Weidenfeld & Nicolson, 1994

Lawson, William, *The Country Housewife's Garden*, 1617

—*The Husbandry of Bees, Published With Secrets Very Necessary For Every Housewife*, 1617

Leyel, Mrs CF, *Green Medicine*, 1937

—*Herbal Delights*, Faber, 1937

Lotions and Potions, National Federation of Women's Institutes, 1968

Loudon, Jane, *Loudon's Lady's Country Companion*, 1845

—*Practical Instructions in Gardening for Ladies*, 1841

Luard, Elizabeth, *European Festival Food*, Bantam, 1990

L'Univers Fantastique des Mythes, Les Presses de la Connaissance, Paris, 1976

Markham, Gervase, *Country Contentments*, 1623

—*The English Hus-wife*, 1615

Mosley, Jane, *Recipes and Remedies 1669–1712*, Derbyshire Museum Service, 1979

Mother Bunch's Closet, 1685

Neumann, E, *The Great Mother*, Routledge, 1996

Opie, Iona and Moira Tatem, *A Dictionary of Superstitions*, Oxford University Press, 1992

Palaiseul, Jean, *Grandmother's Secrets*, Barrie & Jenkins, 1973, reprinted Penguin, 1976

Pisan, Christine de, *The Treasure of the City of Ladies*, 1405, translated by Sarah Lawson, Penguin, 1985

Platt, Sir Hugh, *Delightes for Ladies*, 1605

Pollock, Linda, *With Faith and Physic – The Life of a Tudor Gentlewoman*, Collins & Brown, 1993

Pomeroy, Sarah B, *Goddesses, Whores, Wives and Slaves – Women in Classical Antiquity*, Pimlico, 1994

Radford, E and M, *Encyclopaedia of Superstitions*, edited and revised by Christina Hole, Hutchinson, 1948

Raffald, Elizabeth, *The Experienced English Housekeeper*, 1769

Ratsch, Dr Christian, *A Dictionary of Sacred and Magical Plants*, Prism, 1992

Rohde, Eleanour Sinclair, *The Scented Garden*, Medici Society, 1931

Rundell, Maria, *A New System of Domestic Cookery*, 1807

Saunders, Ann, *The Housekeeping Book of the Saunders Family Women*, manuscript, eighteenth to twentieth centuries, private collection

Smith, Eliza, *The Compleat Housewife*, 1758, published in

facsimile, Studio Editions, 1994

Smith, Mrs, *The Female Economist*, 1810

Spurling, Hilary, ed, *Elinor Fettiplace's Receipt Book*, 1604, Viking Salamander 1986

Thompson, Flora, *Lark Rise to Candleford*, Oxford University Press, 1945

Topsell, Edward, *History of Four-Footed Beasts*, 1607

Tusser, Thomas, *Five Hundredth Pointes of Good Husbandrie*, 1559

Uttley, Alison, *The Country Child*, Faber, 1931

—*Country Things*, Faber, 1946

—*Recipes from an Old Farmhouse*, Faber, 1966

Walker, Barbara G, *The Women's Dictionary of Symbols and Sacred Objects*, Pandora, 1995

—*The Women's Encyclopaedia of Myths and Secrets*, Pandora, 1995

WM, *The Queen's Closet Opened*, 1655

Woolley, Hannah, *The Gentlewoman's Companion*, comprising *The Accomplisht Lady's Delight* and *The Queen-Like Closet*, 1675

Woodward, M, *The Mistress of Stanton's Farm*, Heath Cranton, 1939

The Women's Press is Britain's leading women's publishing house. Established in 1978, we publish high-quality fiction and non-fiction from outstanding women writers worldwide. Our exciting and diverse list includes literary fiction, detective novels, biography and autobiography, health, women's studies, handbooks, literary criticism, psychology and self-help, the arts, our popular Livewire Books series for young women and the bestselling annual *Women Artists Diary* featuring beautiful colour and black-and-white illustrations from the best in contemporary women's art.

If you would like more information about our books or about our mail order book club, please send an A5 sae for our latest catalogue and complete list to:

The Sales Department
The Women's Press Ltd
34 Great Sutton Street
London EC1V 0DX
Tel: 0171 251 3007
Fax: 0171 608 1938